Managing Kubernetes
Operating Kubernetes Clusters in the Real World

Brendan Burns and Craig Tracey

Beijing · Boston · Farnham · Sebastopol · Tokyo

Managing Kubernetes

by Brendan Burns and Craig Tracey

Copyright © 2019 Brendan Burns and Craig Tracey. All rights reserved.

Published by O'Reilly Media, Inc., 1005 Gravenstein Highway North, Sebastopol, CA 95472.

O'Reilly books may be purchased for educational, business, or sales promotional use. Online editions are also available for most titles (*http://oreilly.com/safari*). For more information, contact our corporate/institutional sales department: 800-998-9938 or *corporate@oreilly.com*.

Acquisitions Editor: Nikki McDonald	**Indexer:** WordCo, Inc.
Development Editor: Virginia Wilson	**Interior Designer:** David Futato
Production Editor: Justin Billing	**Cover Designer:** Karen Montgomery
Copyeditor: Shannon Wright	**Illustrator:** Rebecca Demarest
Proofreader: Chris Edwards	

October 2018: First Edition

Revision History for the First Edition
2018-10-05: First Release
2018-11-06: Second Release

See *http://oreilly.com/catalog/errata.csp?isbn=9781492033912* for release details.

The O'Reilly logo is a registered trademark of O'Reilly Media, Inc. *Managing Kubernetes*, the cover image, and related trade dress are trademarks of O'Reilly Media, Inc.

978-1-492-03391-2

[LSI]

Table of Contents

Preface

Who should read This Book

This book is aimed at operators of Kubernetes clusters, either on-premise or in the cloud, or anyone who wants to gain a deeper knowledge of how Kubernetes is architected, installed and maintained. Although there is useful information in this book if you are a Kubernetes user or developer, ultimately this book is lower level than most Kubernetes users will need. Instead it is devoted to the details that concern the people who are responsible for ensuring that a cluster stays healthy, secure and available for developers building applications on Kubernetes.

Why we wrote This Book

While there is an increasingly large body of work both online and in printed form describing how users might best take advantage of Kubernetes to build and deploy their applications, there is relatively little content available for the operators who install, maintain and upgrade Kubernetes clusters. This book steps into that gap and provides a concise collection of the information necessary to successfully operate Kubernetes for yourself or for others.

Kubernetes is ubiquitous today as the most common way people manage containers and build cloud native applications. Indeed Kubernetes as a service is available in all of the major public clouds. But for many people using such a service isn't appealing. Perhaps you have regulatory reasons for preserving data in an on-premise environment like a hospital or financial institution, or perhaps you are operating Kubernetes in a location like a distant airfield or oil platform where limited bandwidth makes using the cloud impossible. Alternately you may simply be interested in gaining the skills needed to run Kubernetes in such an environment.

We hope that the knowledge we have gained through our various experiences operating Kubernetes can be shared through this book. With luck this book will provide you the advantage of our experiences without requiring that you go through the trials and tribulations by which this experience was obtained.

Navigating This Book

This book both summarizes how Kubernetes operates and dives deeply into topics necessary for successfully administering a Kubernetes cluster. After an introduction to the various topics in Chapter 1, Chapters 2 through 5 are devoted to describing the details of the Kubernetes architecture and components. These chapters provide an overview of the various components of Kubernetes and how they come together to implement the Kubernetes API. Additionally, details of how Kubernetes API requests are handled and processed are provided in Chapter 4, while Chapter 5 is devoted to how pods are scheduled into the cluster. A depth of understand of how Kubernetes operates will enable you to better serve your users who will need your help when things go wrong.

The remainder of the book is devoted to specific topics that are required to manage a Kubernetes cluster, including installing and upgrading Kubernetes (Chapter 6) User management, authentication and authorization (Chapters 7–8), admission control (Chapter 9), Kubernetes networking (Chapter 10) and monitoring and disaster recovery (Chapters 11–12). Chapter 13 is devoted to the various ways that the Kubernetes cluster can be extended.

Conventions Used in This Book

The following typographical conventions are used in this book:

Italic
> Indicates new terms, URLs, email addresses, filenames, and file extensions.

`Constant width`
> Used for program listings, as well as within paragraphs to refer to program elements such as variable or function names, databases, data types, environment variables, statements, and keywords.

`Constant width bold`
> Shows commands or other text that should be typed literally by the user.

`Constant width italic`
> Shows text that should be replaced with user-supplied values or by values determined by context.

This element signifies a tip or suggestion.

 This element signifies a general note.

 This element indicates a warning or caution.

Using Code Examples

Supplemental material (code examples, exercises, etc.) is available for download at *https://github.com/managing-kubernetes/managing-kubernetes*.

This book is here to help you get your job done. In general, if example code is offered with this book, you may use it in your programs and documentation. You do not need to contact us for permission unless you're reproducing a significant portion of the code. For example, writing a program that uses several chunks of code from this book does not require permission. Selling or distributing a CD-ROM of examples from O'Reilly books does require permission. Answering a question by citing this book and quoting example code does not require permission. Incorporating a significant amount of example code from this book into your product's documentation does require permission.

We appreciate, but do not require, attribution. An attribution usually includes the title, author, publisher, and ISBN. For example: "*Managing Kubernetes* by Brendan Burns and Craig Tracey (O'Reilly). Copyright 2019 Brendan Burns and Craig Tracey, 978-1-492-03391-2."

If you feel your use of code examples falls outside fair use or the permission given above, feel free to contact us at *permissions@oreilly.com*.

O'Reilly Safari

 *Safari* (formerly Safari Books Online) is a membership-based training and reference platform for enterprise, government, educators, and individuals.

Members have access to thousands of books, training videos, Learning Paths, interactive tutorials, and curated playlists from over 250 publishers, including O'Reilly Media, Harvard Business Review, Prentice Hall Professional, Addison-Wesley Professional, Microsoft Press, Sams, Que, Peachpit Press, Adobe, Focal Press, Cisco Press, John Wiley & Sons, Syngress, Morgan Kaufmann, IBM Redbooks, Packt, Adobe Press, FT Press, Apress, Manning, New Riders, McGraw-Hill, Jones & Bartlett, and Course Technology, among others.

For more information, please visit *http://oreilly.com/safari*.

How to Contact Us

Please address comments and questions concerning this book to the publisher:

O'Reilly Media, Inc.
1005 Gravenstein Highway North
Sebastopol, CA 95472
800-998-9938 (in the United States or Canada)
707-829-0515 (international or local)
707-829-0104 (fax)

We have a web page for this book, where we list errata, examples, and any additional information. You can access this page at *http://bit.ly/managing-kubernetes*.

To comment or ask technical questions about this book, send email to *bookquestions@oreilly.com*.

For more information about our books, courses, conferences, and news, see our website at *http://www.oreilly.com*.

Find us on Facebook: *http://facebook.com/oreilly*

Follow us on Twitter: *http://twitter.com/oreillymedia*

Watch us on YouTube: *http://www.youtube.com/oreillymedia*

Acknowledgments

Brendan would like thank his wonderful family, Robin, Julia, and Ethan for love and support of everything he does. And the Kubernetes community, without whom none of this would be possible.

Craig thanks his family, and especially his wife, who have always supported all of his crazy dreams.

We would both like to thank Scott Collier, Lacie Evenson, Sebastien Goasguen, Erik St. Martin, Jérôme Petazzoni, Ben Straub, and Jason Yee for their feedback on early versions of the manuscript. Thanks also to Nikki McDonald and Virginia Wilson for their work in developing the manuscript and helping us bring all of our ideas together, and to Justin Billing, Shannon Wright, and Chris Edwards for their attention to the finishing touches.

CHAPTER 1
Introduction

Kubernetes is an open source orchestrator for deploying containerized applications. The system was open sourced by Google, inspired by a decade of experience deploying scalable, reliable systems in containers via application-oriented APIs,[1] and developed over the last four years by a vibrant community of open source contributors.

It is used by a large and growing number of developers to deploy reliable distributed systems, as well as to run machine learning, big data, and other batch workloads. A Kubernetes cluster provides an orchestration API that enables applications to be defined and deployed with simple declarative syntax. Further, the Kubernetes cluster itself provides numerous online, self-healing control algorithms that repair applications in the presence of failures. Finally, the Kubernetes API exposes concepts like Deployments that make it easier to perform zero-downtime updates of your software and Service load balancers that make it easy to spread traffic across a number of replicas of your service. Additionally, Kubernetes provides tools for naming and discovery of services so that you can build loosely coupled microservice architectures. Kubernetes is widely used across public and private clouds, as well as physical infrastructure.

This book is dedicated to the topic of managing a Kuberentes cluster. You might be managing your own cluster on your own hardware, part of a team managing a cluster for a larger organization, or a Kubernetes user who wants to go beyond the APIs and learn more about the internals of the system. Regardless of where you are in the journey, deepening your knowledge of how to manage the system can make you more capable of accomplishing all of the things you need to do with Kubernetes.

---

1 Brendan Burns et al., Borg, Omega, and Kubernetes: Lessons Learned from Three Container-Management Systems over a Decade" (*http://bit.ly/2vIrL4S*), *ACM Queue* 14 (2016): 70–93.

When we speak of a *cluster*, we're referring to a collection of machines that work together to provide the aggregate computing power that Kubernetes makes available to its end users. A Kubernetes cluster is a collection of machines that are all controlled by a single API and can be used by consumers of that API.

There are a variety of topics that make up the necessary skills for managing a Kubernetes cluster:

- How the cluster operates
- How to adjust, secure, and tune the cluster
- How to understand your cluster and respond when things go wrong
- How to extend your cluster with new and custom functionality

How the Cluster Operates

Ultimately, if you are going to manage a system, you need to understand how that system operates. What are the pieces that it is made up of, and how do they fit together? Without at least a rough understanding of the components and how they interoperate, you are unlikely to be successful at managing any system. Managing a piece of software, especially one as complex as Kubernetes, without this understanding is like attempting to repair a car without knowing how the tail pipe relates to the engine. It's a bad idea.

However, in addition to understanding how all the pieces fit together, it's also essential to understand how the user consumes the Kubernetes cluster. Only by knowing how a tool like Kubernetes should be used can you truly understand the needs and demands required for its successful management. To revisit our analogy of the car, without understanding the way in which a driver sits in the vehicle and guides it down the road, you are unlikely to successfully manage the vehicle. The same is true of a Kubernetes cluster.

Finally, it is critical that you understand the role that the Kubernetes cluster plays in a user's daily existence. What is the cluster accomplishing for the end user? Which applications are they deploying on it? What complexity and hardship is the cluster removing? What complexity is the Kubernetes API adding? To complete the car analogy, in order to understand the importance of a car to its end user, it is critical to know that it is the thing that ensures a person shows up to work on time. Likewise with Kubernetes, if you don't understand that the cluster is the place where a user's mission-critical application runs, and that the Kubernetes API is what a developer relies on to fix a problem when something goes wrong at 3 a.m., you won't really grasp what is needed to successfully manage that cluster.

Adjust, Secure, and Tune the Cluster

In addition to knowing how the pieces of the cluster fit together and how the Kubernetes API is used by developers to build and deploy applications, it is also critical to understand the various APIs and configuration options to adjust, secure, and tune your cluster. A Kubernetes cluster—or really any significant piece of software—is not something that you simply turn up, start running, and walk away from.

The cluster and its usage have a lifecycle. Developers join and leave teams. New teams are formed and old ones die. The cluster scales with the growth of the business. New Kubernetes releases come out to fix bugs, add new features, and improve stability. Increased demand on the cluster exposes performance problems that had previously been ignored. Responding to all of these changes in the lifespan of your cluster requires an understanding of the ways in which Kubernetes can be configured via command line flags, deployment options, and API configurations.

Additionally, your cluster is not just a target for application deployment. It can also be a vector for attacking the security of your applications. Configuring your cluster to be secure against many different attacks—from application compromises to denial of service—is a critical component of sucessfully managing a cluster. Much of the time, this hardening is, in fact, simply to prevent mistakes. In many cases, the value of hardening and security is that they prevent one team or user from accidentally "attacking" another team's service. However, active attacks do sometimes happen, and the configuration of the cluster is critical to both detecting attacks when they occur and to preventing them from happening in the first place.

Finally, depending on the usage of the cluster, you may need to demonstrate compliance with various security standards that are required for application developers in many industries, such as healthcare, finance, or government. When you understand how to build a compliant cluster, you can put Kubernetes to work in these environments.

Responding When Things Go Wrong

If things never went wrong, it would be a great world to live in. Sadly, of course, that is not the way things are, especially not with any computer system I've ever helped to manage. What's critical when things go wrong is that you learn of it quickly, that you find out through automation and alerts (rather than from a user), and that you are capable of responding and restoring the system as quickly as possible.

The first step in detecting when things break and in understanding why they are broken is to have the right metrics in place. Fortunately, there are two technologies present in the Kubernetes cluster that make this job easier. The first is that Kubernetes itself is generally deployed inside of containers. In addition to the value in reliable packaging and deployment, the container itself forms a boundary where basic metrics such as CPU, memory, network, and disk usage can be observed. These metrics can then be recorded into a monitoring system for both alerting and introspection.

In addition to these container-generated metrics, the Kubernetes codebase itself has been instrumented with a significant number of application metrics. These include things like the number of requests sent or received by various components, as well as the latency of those requests. These metrics are expressed using a format popularized by the Prometheus open source project (*https://prometheus.io*), and they can be easily collected and populated into Prometheus, which can be used directly or with other tools, like Grafana, for visualization and introspection.

Combined together, the baseline metrics from the operating system containers, as well as the application metrics from Kubernetes itself, provide a rich set of data that can be used to generate alerts, which tell you when the system isn't working properly, along with the historical data necessary to debug and determine what went wrong and when.

Of course, understanding the problem is only the first half of the battle. The next step is to respond and recover from the problems with the system. Fortunately, Kubernetes was built in a decoupled, modular manner, with minimal state in the system. This means that, generally, at any given time, it is safe to restart any component in the system that may be overloaded or misbehaving. This modularity and idempotency means that, once you determine the problem, developing a solution is often as straightforward as restarting a few applications.

Of course, in some cases, something truly terrible happens, and, your only recourse is to restore the cluster from a disaster recovery backup somewhere. This presumes that you have enabled such backups in the first place. In addition to all of the monitoring to show you what is happening, the alerts to tell you when something breaks, and the playbooks to tell you how to repair it, successfully managing a cluster requires that you develop and exercise a disaster response and recovery procedure. It's important to remember that simply developing this plan is insufficient. You need to practice it regularly, or you will not be ready (and the plan itself may be flawed) in the presence of a real problem.

Extending the System with New and Custom Functionality

One of the most important strengths of the Kubernetes open source project has been the explosive growth of libraries, tools, and platforms that build on, extend, or otherwise improve the usage of a Kubernetes cluster.

There are tools like Spinnaker or Jenkins for continuous deployment, and tools like Helm that make it easy to package and deploy complete applications. Platforms like Deis provide Git push–style developer workflows, and numerous functions as a service (FaaS) platforms build on top of Kubernetes to enable users to consume it via simple functions. There are even tools for automating the creation and rotation of certificates, in addition to service mesh technologies that make it easy to link and introspect a myriad of microservices.

All of these tools in the ecosystem can be used to enhance, extend, and improve the Kubernetes cluster that you are managing. They can provide new functionality to make your users' lives easier and make the software that they deploy more robust and more manageable.

However, these tools can also make your cluster more unstable, less secure, and more prone to failures. They can expose your users to immature, poorly supported software that feels like an "official" part of the cluster but actually serves to make the users' life more difficult.

Part of managing a Kubernetes cluster is knowing how and when to add these tools, platforms, and projects into the cluster. It requires an exploration and understanding of not only what a particular project is attempting to accomplish but also of the other solutions that exist in the ecosystem. Often, users will come to you with a request for a particular tool based on some video or blog that they happened across. In truth, they are often asking for a capability like continuous integration and continuous delivery (CI/CD) or certificate rotation.

It is your job as a cluster manager to act as a curator of such projects. You are also an editor and an advisor who can recommend alternate solutions or determine whether a particular project is a good fit for your cluster or if there is a better way of accomplishing the same goal for the end user.

Additionally, the Kubernetes API itself contains rich tools for extending and enhancing the API. A Kubernetes cluster is not limited solely to the APIs that are built into it. Instead, new APIs can be dynamically added and removed. Besides the existing extensions just mentioned, sometimes the job of managing a Kubernetes cluster involves developing new code and new extensions that enhance your cluster in ways that were previously impossible. Part of managing a cluster may very well be developing new tooling. Of course, once developed, sharing that tooling with the growing Kubernetes ecosystem is a great way to give back to the community that brought you the Kubernetes software in the first place.

Summary

Managing a Kubernetes cluster is more than just the act of installing some software on a set of machines. Successful management requires a solid grasp of how Kubernetes is put together and how it is put to use by the developers who are Kubernetes users. It requires that you understand how to maintain, adjust, and improve the cluster over time as its usage patterns change. Additionally, you need to know how to monitor the information put off by the cluster in operation and how to develop the alerts and dashboards to tell you when the cluster is sick and how to make it healthy again. Finally, you need to understand when and how to extend the Kubernetes cluster with other tools to make it even more helpful to your users. We hope that within this book you find answers and more for all of these topics and that, at completion, you find yourself with the skills to be successful at *Managing Kubernetes*.

## CHAPTER 2

An Overview of Kubernetes

Building, deploying, and managing applications on top of the Kubernetes API is a complex topic in its own right. It is beyond the scope of this book to give a complete understanding of the Kubernetes API in all of its detail. For those purposes, there are a number of books, such as *Kubernetes: Up and Running* (*http://http://bit.ly/ kubernetes-up-and-running*) (O'Reilly), and online resources that will give you the knowledge necessary to build an application on Kubernetes. If you are completely new to Kubernetes and interested in building applications on top of the system, we definitely recommend taking advantage of these resources to augment the information in this chapter.

On the other hand, if you are responsible for managing a Kubernetes cluster or you have a high-level understanding of the Kubernetes API, this chapter provides an introduction to the basic concepts of Kubernetes and their role in the development of an application. If after reading this chapter you still feel uncomfortable having a conversation with your users about their use of Kubernetes, we highly recommend that you avail yourself of these additional resources.

In this chapter, we first introduce the notion of containers and how they can be used to package and deploy your application. Then we introduce the core concepts behind the Kubernetes API, and finally, we conclude with some higher-level concepts that Kubernetes has added to make specific tasks easier.

Containers

Containers were popularized by Docker and enabled a revolution in the way in which developers package and deploy their applications. However, along the way, the very word *container* has taken on many different meanings to many different people.

Because Kubernetes is a *container orchestrator* to understand Kubernetes, it's important to understand what we mean when we say *container*.

In reality, a container is made up of two different pieces, and a group of associated features. A container includes:

- A container image
- A set of operating system concepts that isolates a running process or processes

The *container image* contains the application runtime, which consists of binaries, libraries, and other data needed to run the container. Developer can package up their application as a container image on their development laptop and have faith that when that image is deployed and run in a different setting—be it another user's laptop or a server in a datacenter—the container will behave exactly as it did on the developer's laptop. This portability and consistent execution in a variety of environments are among the primary values of container images.

When a container image is run, it is also executed using namespaces in the operating system. These namespaces contain the process and provide isolation for it and its peers from other things running on the machine. This isolation means, for example, that each running container has its own separated filesystem (like a chroot). Additionally, each container has its own network and PID namespaces, meaning that process number 42 in one container is a different process than number 42 in another container. There are many other namespaces within the kernel that separate various running containers from each other. Additionally, control groups (cgroups) allow the isolation of resource usage, like memory or CPU. Finally, standard operating system security features, like SELinux or AppArmor, can also be used with running containers. Combined, all of this isolation makes it more difficult for different processes running in separate containers to interfere with each other.

 When we say *isolation*, it is incredibly important to know that this is in terms of resources, like CPU, memory, or files. Containers as implemented in Linux and Windows do *not* currently provide strong security isolation for different processes. Containers when combined with other kernel-level isolation can provide reasonable security isolation for some use cases. However, in the general case, only hypervisor-level security is strong enough to isolate truly hostile workloads.

In order to make all of this work, a number of different tools were created to help build and deploy containerized applications.

The first is the container image builder. Typically the docker command-line tool is used to build a container image. However, the image format has been standardized through the Open Container Initiative (OCI) standard. This has enabled the development of other image builders, available via cloud API, CI/CD, or new alternative tools and libraries.

The docker tool uses a *Dockerfile*, which specifies a set of instructions for how to construct the container image. Full details on using the docker tool are beyond the scope of this book, but there are numerous resources available in books like *Docker: Up and Running* (*http://bit.ly/docker-up-running-2e*) (O'Reilly) or in online resources. If you have never built a container image before, put down this book right now, go read about containers, and come back when you have built a few container images.

After a container image has been built, we need a way to distribute that image from a user's laptop up to other users, the cloud, or a private datacenter. This is where the *image registry* comes in. The image registry is an API for uploading and managing images. After an image has been built, it is pushed to the image registry. After the image is in the registry, it can be pulled, or downloaded, from that registry to any machine that has access to the registry. Every registry requires some form of authorization to push an image, but some registries are *public*, meaning that once an image is pushed, anyone in the world can pull and start running the image. Others are *private* and require authorization to pull an image, as well. At this point, there are registries as a service available from every public cloud, and there are open source registry servers, which you can download and run in your own environment. Before you even begin to set up your Kubernetes cluster, it's a good idea to figure out where you are going to store the images that you run in it.

Once you have packaged your application as a container image and pushed it to a registry, it's time to use that container to deploy the application, and that's where container orchestration comes in.

Container Orchestration

After you have a container image stored in a registry somewhere, you need to run it to create a working application. This is where a container orchestrator like Kubernetes comes into the picture. Kuberentes' job is to take a group of machines that provide resources, like CPU, memory, and disk, and transform them into a container-oriented API that developers can use to deploy their containers.

The Kubernetes API enables you to declare you desired state of the world, for example, "I want this container image to run, and it needs 3 cores and 10 gigabytes of memory to run correctly." The Kubernetes system then reviews its fleet of machines, finds a good place for that container image to run, and *schedules* the execution of that container on that machine. Developers see their container image running, and more often than not, they don't need to concern themselves with the specific location where their container is executing.

Of course, running just a single container is neither that interesting nor that reliable, so the Kubernetes API also provides easy ways to say, "I want three copies of this container image running on different machines, each with 3 cores and 10 gigabytes of memory."

But the orchestration system is about more than scheduling containers to machines. In addition to that, the Kubernetes orchestrator knows how to heal those containers if they fail. If the process inside your container crashes, Kubernetes restarts it. If you define custom health checks, Kubernetes can use them to determine whether your application is deadlocked and needs to be restarted (*liveness checks*) or if it should be part of a load-balanced service (*readiness checks*).

Speaking of load balancing, Kubernetes also provides API objects for defining a way to load balance traffic between these various replicas. It provides a way to say, "Please create this load balancer to represent these running containers." These load balancers are also given easy-to-discover names so that linking different services together within a cluster is easy.

Kubernetes also has objects that perform zero-downtime rollouts and that manage configurations, persistent volumes, secrets, and much more. The following sections detail the specific objects in the Kubernetes API that make all of this possible.

The Kubernetes API

The Kubernetes API is a RESTful API based on HTTP and JSON and provided by an *API server*. All of the components in Kubernetes communicate through the API. This architecture is covered in more detail in Chapter 3. As an open source project, the Kubernetes API is always evolving, but the core objects have been stable for years and the Kubernetes community provides a strong deprecation policy that ensures that developers and operators don't have to change what they are doing with each revision of the system. Kubernetes provides an OpenAPI specification for the API, as well as numerous client libraries in a variety of languages (*https://github.com/kubernetes-client*).

Basic Objects: Pods, ReplicaSets, and Services

Although it has a large and growing number of objects in its API, Kubernetes began with a relatively small number of objects, and these are still the core of what Kubernetes does.

Pods

A *Pod* is the atomic unit of scheduling in a Kubernetes cluster. A Pod is made up of a collection of one or more running containers. (A Pod is a collection of whales, derived from Docker's whale logo.) When we say that a Pod is *atomic*, what we mean is that all of the containers in a Pod are guaranteed to land on the same machine in the cluster. Pods also share many resources between the containers. For example, they all share the same network namespace, which means that each container in a Pod can see the other containers in the Pod on localhost. Pods also share the process and interprocess communication namespaces so that different containers can use tools, like shared memory and signaling, to coordinate between the different processes in the Pod.

This close grouping means that Pods are ideally suited for symbiotic relationships between their containers, such as a main serving container and a background data-loading container. Keeping the container images separate generally makes it more agile for different teams to own or reuse the container images, but grouping them together in a Pod at runtime enables them to operate cooperatively.

When people first encounter Pods in Kubernetes, they sometimes spring to the wrong assumptions. For example, a user may see a Pod and think, "Ah yes, a frontend and a database server make up a Pod." But this is generally the wrong level of granularity. To see why, consider that the Pod is also the unit of scaling and replication, which means that, if you group your frontend and your database in the same container, you will replicate your database at the same rate that you replicate your frontends. It is unlikely that you want to do things this way.

Pods also do things to keep your application running. If the process in a container crashes, Kubernetes automatically restarts it. Pods can also define application-level health checks that can provide a richer, application-specific way of determining whether the Pod should be automatically restarted.

ReplicaSets

Of course, if you are deploying a container orchestrator just to run individual containers, you are probably overcomplicating your life. In general, one of the main reasons for container orchestration is to make it easier to build replicated, reliable systems. Although individual containers may fail or may be incapable of serving the load of a system, replicating an application out to a number of different running containers dramatically reduces the probability that your service will completely fail at a particular moment in time. Plus, horizontal scaling enables you to grow your application in response to load. In the Kubernetes API, this sort of stateless replication is handled by a ReplicaSet object. A ReplicaSet ensures that, for a given Pod definition, a number of replicas exists within the system. The actual replication is handled by the Kubernetes controller manager, which creates Pod objects that are scheduled by the Kubernetes scheduler. These details of the architecture are described in later chapters.

ReplicaSet is a newer object. At its v1 release, Kubernetes had an API object called a ReplicationController. Due to the deprecation policy, ReplicationControllers continue to exist in the Kubernetes API, but their usage is strongly discouraged in favor of ReplicaSets.

Services

After you can replicate your application out using a replica set, the next logical goal is to create a load balancer to spread traffic to these different replicas. To accomplish this, Kubernetes has a Service object. A Service represents a TCP or UDP load-balanced service. Every Service that is created, whether TCP or UDP, gets three things:

- Its own IP address
- A DNS entry in the Kubernetes cluster DNS
- Load-balancing rules that proxy traffic to the Pods that implement the Service

When a Service is created, it is assigned a fixed IP address. This IP address is virtual —it does not correspond to any interface present on the network. Instead, it is programmed into the network fabric as a load-balanced IP address. When packets are sent to that IP, they are load balanced out to a set of Pods that implements the Service. The load balancing that is performed can either be round robin or deterministic, based on source and destination IP address tuples.

Given this fixed IP address, a DNS name is programmed into the Kubernetes cluster's DNS server. This DNS address provides a semantic name (e.g., "frontend"), which is the same as the name of the Kubernetes Service object and which enables other containers in the cluster to discover the IP address of the Service load balancer.

Finally, the Service load balancing is programmed into the network fabric of the Kubernetes cluster so that any container that tries to talk to the Service IP address is correctly load balanced to the corresponding Pods. This programming of the network fabric is dynamic, so as Pods come and go due to failures or scaling of a ReplicaSet, the load balancer is constantly reprogrammed to match the current state of the cluster. This means that clients can rely on connections to the Service IP address always resolving to a Pod that implements the Service.

Storage: Persistent Volumes, ConfigMaps, and Secrets

A common question that comes up after an initial exploration of Kubernetes is, "What about my files?" With all of these containers coming and going within the cluster and landing on different machines, it's difficult to understand how you should manage the files and storage you want to be associated with your containers. Fortunately, Kubernetes provides several different API objects to help you manage your files.

The first storage concept introduced in Kubernetes was Volume, which is actually a part of the Pod API. Within a Pod, you can define a set of Volumes. Each Volume can be one of a large number of different types. At present, there are more than 10 different types of Volumes you can create, including NFS, iSCSI, gitRepo, cloud storage–based Volumes, and more.

 Though the Volume interface was initially a point of extensibility via writing code within Kubernetes, the explosion of different Volume types eventually showed how unsustainable this model was. Now, new Volume types are developed outside of the Kubernetes code and use the Container Storage Interface (CSI), an interface for storage that is independent of Kubernetes.

When you add a Volume to your Pod, you can choose to mount it to an arbitrary location in each running container. This enables your running container to have access to the storage within the Volume. Different containers can mount these Volumes at different locations or can ignore the Volume entirely.

In addition to basic files, there are several types of Kubernetes objects that can themselves be mounted into your Pod as a Volume. The first of these is the ConfigMap object. A ConfigMap represents a collection of configuration files. In Kubernetes, you want to have different configurations for the same container image. When you add a ConfigMap-based Volume to your Pod, the files in the ConfigMap show up in the specified directory in your running container.

Kubernetes uses the Secret configuration type for secure data, such as database passwords and certificates. In the context of Volumes, a Secret works identically to a ConfigMap. It can be attached to a Pod via a Volume and mounted into a running container for use.

Over time, deploying applications with Volumes revealed that the tight binding of Volumes to Pods was actually problematic. For example, when creating a replicated container (via a ReplicaSet) the same exact volume must be used by all replicas. In many situations, this is acceptable, but in some cases, you migth want a different Volume for each replica. Additionally, specifying a precise volume type (e.g., an Azure disk-persistent Volume) binds your Pod definition to a specific environment (in this case, the Microsoft Azure cloud), but it is often desirable to have a Pod definition that requests a generic type of storage (e.g., 10 gigabytes of network storage) without specifying a provider. To accomplish this, Kubernetes introduced the notion of PersistentVolumes and PersistentVolumeClaims. Instead of binding a Volume directly into a Pod, a PersistentVolume is created as a separate object. This object is then claimed to a specific Pod by a `PersistentVolumeClaim` and finally mounted into the Pod via this claim. At first, this seems overly complicated, but the abstraction of Volume and Pod enables both the portability and automatic volume creation required by the two previous use cases.

Organizing Your Cluster with Namespaces, Labels, and Annotations

The Kubernetes API makes it quite easy to create a large number of objects in the system, but such a collection of objects can easily make administering a cluster a nightmare. Fortunately, Kubernetes also has many objects that make it easier to manage, query, and reason about the objects in your cluster.

Namespaces

The first object for organizing your cluster is `Namespace`. You can think of a `Namespace` as something like a folder for your Kubernetes API objects. `Namespaces` provide directories for containing most of the other objects in the cluster. `Namespaces` can also provide a scope for role-based access control (RBAC) rules. Like a folder, when you delete a `Namespace`, all of the objects within it are also destroyed, so be careful! Every Kubernetes cluster has a single built-in `Namespace` named `default`, and most installations of Kubernetes also include a `Namespace` named `kube-system`, where cluster administration containers are created.

 Kubernetes objects are divided into *namespaced* and *non-namespaced* objects, depending on whether they can be placed in a `Namespace`. Most common Kubernetes API objects are namespaced objects. But some objects that apply to an entire cluster (e.g., `Namespace` objects themselves, or cluster-level RBAC), are not namespaced.

In addition to organizing Kubernetes objects, `Namespaces` are also placed into the DNS names created for `Services` and the DNS search paths that are provided to containers. The complete DNS name for a `Service` is something like *my-service.svc.my-namespace.cluster.internal*, which means that two different `Services` in different `Namespaces` will end up with different fully qualified domain names (FQDNs). Additionally, the DNS search paths for each container include the `Namespace`, thus a DNS lookup for `frontend` will be translated to *frontend.svc.foo.cluster.internal* for a container in the `foo` `Namespace` and *frontend.svc.bar.cluster.internal* for a container in the `bar` `Namespace`.

Labels and label queries

Every object in the Kubernetes API can have an arbitrary set of *labels* associated with it. Labels are string key-value pairs that help identify the object. For example, a label might be "role": "frontend", which indicates that the object is a frontend. These labels can be used to query and filter objects in the API. For example, you can request that the API server provide you with a list of all Pods where the label role is backend. These requests are called *label queries* or *label selectors*. Many objects within the Kubernetes API use label selectors as a way to identify sets of objects that they apply to. For example, a Pod can have a *node selector*, which identifies the set of nodes on which the Pod is elegible to run (nodes with GPUs, for example). Likewise, a Service has a *Pod selector*, which identifies the set of Pods that the Service should load balance traffic to. Labels and label selectors are the fundamental manner in which Kubernetes loosely couples its objects together.

Annotations

Not every metadata value that you want to assign to an API object is identifying information. Some of the information is simply an *annotation* about the object itself. Thus every Kubernetes API object can also have arbitrary annotations. These might include something like the icon to display next to the object or a modifier that changes the way that the object is interpreted by the system.

Often, experimental or vendor-specific features in Kubernetes are initially implemented using annotations, since they are not part of the formal API specification. In these cases, the annotation itself should carry some notion of the stability of the feature (e.g., beta.kubernetes.io/activate-some-beta-feature).

Advanced Concepts: Deployments, Ingress, and StatefulSets

Of course, simple, replicated, load-balanced Services are not the only style of application that you might want to deploy in containers. And, as Kubernetes has evolved, it has added new API objects to better suit more specialized use cases, including improved rollouts, HTTP-based load balancing and routing, and stateful workloads.

Deployments

Although ReplicaSets are the primitive for running many different copies of the same container image, applications are not static entities. They evolve as developers add new features and fix bugs. This means that the act of rolling out new code to a Service is as important a feature as replicating it to reliably handle load.

The Deployment object was added to the Kubernetes API to represent this sort of safe rollout from one version to another. A Deployment can hold pointers to multiple Rep licaSets, (e.g., v1 and v2), and it can control the slow and safe migration from one ReplicaSet to another.

To understand how a Deployment works, imagine that you have an application that is deployed to three replicas in a ReplicaSet named rs-v1. When you ask a Deployment to roll out a new image (v2), the Deployment creates a new ReplicaSet (rs-v2) with a single replica. The Deployment waits for this replica to becomes healthy, and when it is, the Deployment reduces the number of replicas in rs-v1 to two. It then increases the number of replicas in rs-v2 to two also, and waits for the second replica of v2 to become healthy. This process continues until there are no more replicas of v1 and there are three healthy replicas of v2.

 Deployments feature a large number of different knobs that can be tuned to provide a safe rollout for the specific details of an application. Indeed, in most modern clusters, users exclusively use Deployment objects and don't manage ReplicaSets directly.

HTTP load balancing with Ingress

Although Service objects provide a great way to do simple TCP-level load balancing, they don't provide an application-level way to do load balancing and routing. The truth is that most of the applications that users deploy using containers and Kubernetes are HTTP web-based applications. These are better served by a load balancer that understands HTTP. To address these needs, the Ingress API was added to Kubernetes. Ingress represents a path and host-based HTTP load balancer and router. When you create an Ingress object, it receives a virtual IP address just like a Service, but instead of the one-to-one relationship between a Service IP address and a set of Pods, an Ingress can use the content of an HTTP request to route requests to different Services.

To get a clearer understanding of how Ingress works, imagine that we have two Kubernetes Services named "foo" and "bar." Each has its own IP address, but we really want to expose them to the internet as part of the same host. For example, *foo.company.com* and *bar.company.com*. We can do this by creating an Ingress object and associating its IP address with both the *foo.company.com* and *bar.company.com* DNS names. In the Ingress object, we also map the two different hostnames to the two different Kubernetes Services. That way, when a request for *https:/ / foo.company.com* is received, it is routed to the "foo" Service in the cluster, and similarly for *https://bar.company.com*. With Ingress, the routing can be based on either host or path or both, so *https://company.com/bar* can also be routed to the "bar" Service.

The Ingress API is one of the most decoupled and flexible APIs in Kubernetes. By default, although Kubernetes will store Ingress objects, nothing happens when they are created. Instead, you need to also run an *Ingress Controller* in the cluster to take appropriate action when the Ingress object is created. One of the most popular Ingress Controllers is nginx, but there are numerous implementations that use other HTTP load balancers or that use cloud or physical load-balancer APIs.

StatefulSets

Most applications operate correctly when replicated horizontally and treated as identical clones. Each replica has no unique identity independent of any other. For representing such applications, a Kubernetes ReplicaSet is the perfect object. However, some applications, especially stateful storage workloads or sharded applications, require more differentiation between the replicas in the application. Although it is possible to add this differentiation at the application level on top of a ReplicaSet, doing so is complicated, error prone, and repetitive for end users.

To resolve this, Kubernetes has recently introduced StatefulSets as a complement to ReplicaSets, but for more stateful workloads. Like ReplicaSets, StatefulSets create multiple instances of the same container image running in a Kubernetes cluster, but the manner in which containers are created and destroyed is more deterministic, as are the names of each container.

In a ReplicaSet, each replicated Pod receives a name that involves a random hash (e.g., *frontend-14a2*), and there is no notion of ordering in a ReplicaSet. In contrast, with StatefulSets, each replica receives a monotonically increasing index (e.g., *backed-0, backend-1*, and so on).

Further, StatefulSets guarantee that replica zero will be created and become healthy before replica one is created and so forth. When combined, this means that applications can easily bootstrap themselves using the initial replica (e.g., *backend-0*) as a bootstrap master. All subsequent replicas can rely on the fact that *backend-0* has to exist. Likewise, when replicas are removed from a StatefulSet, they are removed at the highest index. If a StatefulSet is scaled down from five to four replicas, it is guaranteed that the fifth replica is the one that will be removed.

Additionally, StatefulSets receive DNS names so that each replica can be accessed directly, in addition to the complete StatefulSet. This allows clients to easily target specific shards in a sharded service.

Batch Workloads: Job and ScheduledJob

In addition to stateful workloads, another specialized class of workloads are *batch* or *one-time workloads*. In contrast to the previously discussed workloads, these are not constantly serving traffic. Instead, they perform some computation and are then destroyed when the computation is complete.

In Kubernetes, a `Job` represents a set of tasks that needs to be run. Like `ReplicaSets` and `StatefulSets`, `Jobs` operate by creating Pods to execute work by running container images. However, unlike `ReplicaSets` and `StatefulSets`, the Pods created by a `Job` only run until they complete and exit. A `Job` contains the definition of the Pods it creates, the number of times the `Job` should be run, and the maximum number of Pods to create in parallel. For example, a `Job` with 100 repetitions and a maximum parallelism of 10 will run 10 Pods simultaneously, creating new Pods as old ones complete, until there have been 100 successful executions of the container image.

`ScheduledJobs` build on top of the `Job` object by adding a schedule to a `Job`. A `ScheduledJob` contains the definition of the `Job` object that you want to create, as well as the schedule on which that `Job` should be created.

Cluster Agents and Utilities: DaemonSets

One of the most common questions that comes up when people are moving to Kubernetes is, "How do I run my machine agents?" Examples of agents' tasks include intrusion detection, logging and monitoring, and others. Many people attempt non-Kubernetes approaches to enable these agents, such as adding new systemd unit files or initialization scripts. Although these approaches can work, they have several downsides. The first is that Kubernetes does not include agents' activity in its accounting of resources in use on the cluster. The second is that container images and Kubernetes APIs for health checking, monitoring, and more cannot be applied to these agents. Fortunately, Kubernetes makes the `DaemonSet` API available to users to install such agents on their clusters. A `DaemonSet` provides a template for a Pod that should be run on every machine. When a `DaemonSet` is created, Kubernetes ensures that this Pod is running on each node in the cluster. If, at some later point, a new node is added, Kubernetes creates a Pod on that node, as well. Although by default Kubernetes places a Pod on every node in the cluster, a `DaemonSet` can also provide a node selector label query, and Kubernetes will only place that `DaemonSet`'s Pods onto nodes that match that label query.

Summary

The goal of this book is to teach you how to successfully manage a Kubernetes cluster. But to successfully manage any service, you need to understand what that service makes available to the end user, as well as how the user uses the service. In this case, we are delivering a reliable Kubernetes API to developers. Developers, in turn, are using this API to successfully build and deploy their applications. Understanding the various parts of the Kubernetes API will enable you to understand your end users and to do a better job of managing the system that they rely on for their daily activities. This chapter is really an abbreviated summary of topics that are covered in much longer books, like *Kubernetes: Up and Running* (*http://http://bit.ly/kubernetes-up-and-running*) (O'Reilly), as well as on the core Kubernetes website (*https://kubernetes.io*). Readers who are interested in going more deeply into the Kubernetes API are strongly encouraged to learn more from these resources.

Kubernetes Architecture

Although Kubernetes is intended to make it easier to deploy and manage distributed systems, Kubernetes itself is a distributed system that needs to be managed. To be able to do that, a developer needs to have a strong understanding of the system architecture, the role of each piece in the system, and how they all fit together.

Concepts

To understand the architecture of Kubernetes, it is helpful, at first, to have a good grasp of the concepts and design principals that govern its development. Although the system can seem quite complex, it is actually based on a relatively small number of concepts that are repeated throughout. This allows Kubernetes to grow, while still remaining approachable to developers. Knowledge about one component in the system often can be directly applied to others.

Declarative Configuration

The notion of *declarative configuration*—when a user declares a desired state of the world to produce a result—is one of the primary drivers behind the development of Kubernetes. For example, a user might say to Kubernetes, "I want there to be five replicas of my web server running at all times." Kubernetes, in turn, takes that declarative statement and takes responsibility for ensuring that it is true. Unfortunately, Kubernetes is unable to understand natural language instructions and so that declaration is actually in the form of a structured YAML or JSON document.

Declarative configuration differs from *imperative configuration* in which users take a series of direct actions (e.g., creating each of the five replicas that they want to have up and running). Imperative actions are often simpler to understand—one can simply say, "run this," instead of using a more complex declarative syntax. However, the power of the declarative approach is that you are giving the system more than a sequence of instructions—you are giving it a declaration of your desired state. Because Kubernetes understands your desired state, it can take autonomous action, independent of user interaction. This means that it can implement automatic self-correcting and self-healing behaviors. For a developer, this is critical, since it means that the system can fix itself without waking you up in the middle of the night.

Reconciliation or Controllers

To achieve these self-healing or self-correcting behaviors, Kubernetes is structured based on a large number of *independent reconciliation* or *control loops*. When designing a system like Kubernetes, there are generally two different approaches that you can take—a monolithic state-based approach or a decentralized controller–based approach.

In *monolithic system design*, the system is aware of the entire state of the world and uses this complete view to move everything forward in a coordinated fashion. This can be very attractive, since the operation of the system is centralized and thus easier to understand. The problem with the monolithic approach is that it is not particularly stable. If anything unexpected happens, the entire system can come crashing down.

Kubernetes takes an alternative *decentralized approach* in its design. Instead of a single monolithic controller, Kubernetes is composed of a large number of controllers, each performing its own independent reconciliation loop. Each individual loop is only responsible for a small piece of the system (e.g., updating the list of endpoints for a particular load balancer), and each small controller is wholly unaware of the rest of the world. This focus on a small problem and the corresponding ignorance of the broader state of the world makes the entire system significantly more stable. Each controller is largely independent of all others and thus unaffected by problems or changes unrelated to itself. The downside, though, of this distributed approach is that the overall behavior of the system can be harder to understand, since there is no single location to look for an explanation of why the system is behaving the way that it is. Instead, it is necessary to look at the interoperation of a large number of independent processes.

The control loop design pattern makes Kubernetes more flexible and stable and is repeated throughout Kubernetes' system components. The basic idea behind a control loop is that it is continually repeating the following steps, as shown in Figure 3-1:

1. Obtain the desired state of the world.
2. Observe the world.
3. Find differences between the observation of the world and the desired state of the world.

4. Take actions to make the observation of the world match the desired state.

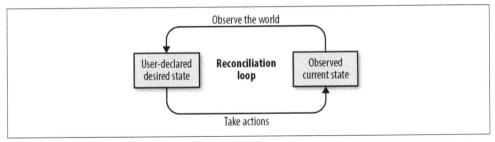

Figure 3-1. An illustration of a generic reconciliation loop

The easiest example to help you understand the operation of a reconciliation control loop is the thermostat in your home. It has a desired state (the temperature that you entered on the thermostat), it makes observations of the world (the current temperature of your house), it finds the difference between these values, and it then takes actions (either heating or cooling) to make the real world match the desired state of the world.

The controllers in Kubernetes do the same thing. They observe the desired state of the world via the declarative statements that are made to the Kubernetes API server. For example, a user might declare, "I want four replicas of that web server." The Kubernetes replication controller takes this desired state and then observes the world. It might see that there are currently three replicas of the web-serving container. The controller finds the difference between the current and desired state (one missing web server) and then takes action to make the current state match the desired state by creating a fourth web-serving container.

Of course, one of the challenges of managing this declarative state is determining the set of web servers that the reconciliation control loop should be paying attention to. This is where labels and label queries enter the Kubernetes design.

Implicit or Dynamic Grouping

Whether it is grouping together a set of replicas or identifying the backends for a load balancer, there are numerous times in the implementation of Kubernetes when it is necessary to identify a set of things. When grouping things together into a set, there are two possible approaches—*explicit/static* or *implicit/dynamic grouping*. With static grouping, every group is defined by a concrete list (e.g., "The members of my team are Alice, Bob, and Carol."). The list explicitly calls out the name of each member of the group, and the list is static—that is, the membership doesn't change unless the list itself changes. Much like a monolithic approach to design, this static grouping is easily understandable. To know who is in a group, one simply has to read the list. The challenge with static grouping is that it is inflexible—it cannot respond to a dynamically changing world. Hopefully, at this point, you know that Kubernetes uses a more dynamic approach to grouping. In Kubernetes, groups are implicitly defined.

The alternative to explicit, static groups is implicit, dynamic groups. With implicit groups, instead of the list of members, the group is defined by a statement like, "The members of my team are the people wearing orange." This group is implicitly defined. Nowhere in the definition of the group are the members defined; instead, they are implied by evaluating the group definition against a set of people who are present. Because the set of people who are present can always change, the membership of the group is likewise dynamic and changing. Although this can introduce complexity, because of the second step (in the example case, looking for people wearing orange), it is also significantly more flexible and stable, and it can handle a changing environment without requiring constant adjustments to static lists.

In Kubernetes, this implicit grouping is achieved via labels and label queries or label selectors. Every API object in Kubernetes can have an arbitrary number of key/value pairs called "labels" that are associated with the object. You can then use a label query or label selector to identify a set of objects that matches that query. A concrete example of this is shown in Figure 3-2.

 Every Kubernetes object has both labels and annotations. Initially they might seem redundant, but their uses are different. Labels can be queried and should provide information that serves to identify the object in some way. Annotations cannot be queried and should be used for general metadata about the object—metadata that doesn't represent its identity (e.g., the icon to display next to the object when it is rendered graphically).

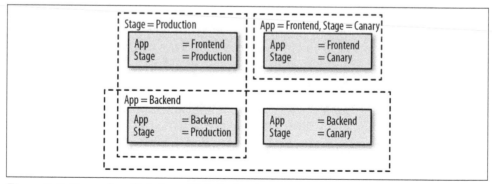

Figure 3-2. Examples of labels and label selection

Structure

Now that you have some sense of the design concepts that are implemented in the Kubernetes system, let's consider the design principles used to build Kubernetes. The following fundamental design tenets are critical in Kubernetes development.

Unix Philosophy of Many Components

Kubernetes ascribes to the general Unix philosophy of modularity and of small pieces that do their jobs well. Kubernetes is not a single monolithic application that implements all of the various functionality in a single binary. Instead, it is a collection of different applications that all work together, largely ignorant of each other, to implement the overall system known as Kubernetes. Even when there is a binary (e.g., the controller manager) that groups together a large number of different functions, those functions are held almost entirely independently from each other in that binary. They are compiled together largely to make the task of deploying and managing Kubernetes easier, not because of any tight binding between the components.

Again, the advantage of this modular approach is that Kubernetes is flexible. Large pieces of functionality can be ripped out and replaced without the rest of the system noticing or caring. The downside, of course, is the complexity, since deploying, monitoring, and understanding the system requires integrating information and configuration across a number of different tools. Sometimes these pieces are compiled into a single binary executable, but even when this occurs, they still communicate through the API server rather than directly within the running process.

API-Driven Interactions

The second structural design within Kubernetes is that all interaction between components is driven through a centralized API surface area. An important corollary of this design is that the API that the components use is the exact same API used by every other cluster user. This has two important consequences for Kubernetes. The first is that no part of the system is more privileged or has more direct access to internals than any other. Indeed, with the exception of the API server that implements the API, no one has access to the internals at all. Thus, every component can be swapped for an alternative implementation, and new functionality can be added without rearchitecting the core components. As we will see in later chapters, even core components like the scheduler can be swapped out and replaced (or merely augmented) with alternative implementations.

The API-driven interactions incentivize a system to be stably designed in the presence of version skew. When you roll out a distributed system to a grouping of machines, for a period of time, you will have both the older version and the new version of the software running simultaneously. If you haven't planned directly for this version skew, the unplanned (and often untested) interactions between old and new versions can cause instability and outages. Because in Kubernetes everything is mediated through the API and the API provides strongly defined API versions and conversion between different version numbers, the problems of version skew can largely be avoided. In reality, though, occasional problems can still crop up, and version skew and upgrade testing is an important part of Kubernetes release qualification.

Components

With knowledge of both the concepts and structures in the Kubernetes architecture, we can now discuss the individual components that make up Kubernetes. This is a glossary of sorts—a world map that you can refer to when you need an overview of how the various pieces of the Kubernetes system fit together. Some of the components are more important than others, and thus are covered in much more detail in later chapters, but this reference guide will help ground and contextualize those later explorations.

Kubernetes is a system that groups together a large fleet of machines into a single unit that can be consumed via an API, but the implementation of Kubernetes actually subdivides the set of machines into two groups: worker nodes and head nodes. Most of the components that make up the Kubernetes infrastructure run on *head* or *control plane* nodes. There are a limited number of such nodes in a cluster, generally one, three, or five. These nodes run the components that implement Kubernetes, like etcd and the API server. There is an odd number of these nodes, since they need to keep quorum in a shared state using a Raft/Paxos algorithm for quorum. The cluster's actual work is done on the worker nodes. These nodes also run a more limited selection of Kubernetes components. Finally, there are Kubernetes components that are scheduled to the Kubernetes cluster after it is created. From a Kubernetes perspective, these components are indistinguishable from other workloads, but they do implement part of the overall Kubernetes API.

The following discussion of the Kubernetes components breaks them into three groupings: the components that run on head nodes, the components that run on all nodes, and the components that run scheduled onto the cluster.

Head Node Components

A head node is the brain of the Kubernetes cluster. It contains a collection of core components that implement the Kubernetes API functionality. Typically, only these components run on head nodes; there are no user containers that share these nodes.

etcd

The *etcd system* is at the heart of any Kubernetes cluster. It implements the key-value stores where all of the objects in a Kubernetes cluster are persisted. The etcd servers implement a distributed consensus algorithm, namely Raft, which ensures that even if one of the storage servers fails, there is sufficient replication to maintain the data stored in etcd and to recover data when an etcd server becomes healthy again and re-adds itself to the cluster. The etcd servers also provide two other important pieces of functionality that Kubernetes makes heavy use of. The first is optimistic concurrency. Every value stored in etcd has a corresponding resource version. When a key-value pair is written to an etcd server, it can be conditionalized on a particular resource version. This means that, using etcd, you can implement *compare and swap*, which is at the core of any concurrency system. Compare and swap enables a user to read a value and update it knowing that no other component in the system has also updated the value. These assurances enable the system to safely have multiple threads manipulating data in etcd without the need for pessimistic locks, which can significantly reduce throughput to the server.

In addition to implementing compare and swap, the etcd servers also implement a *watch* protocol. The value of watch is that it enables clients to efficiently watch for changes in the key-value stores for an entire directory of values. As an example, all objects in a Namespace are stored within a directory in etcd. The use of a watch enables a client to efficiently wait for and react to changes without continuous polling of the etcd server.

API server

Although etcd is at the core of a Kubernetes cluster, there is actually only a single server that is allowed to have direct access to the Kubernetes cluster, and that is the API server. The API server is the hub of the Kubernetes cluster; it mediates all interactions between clients and the API objects stored in etcd. Consequently, it is the central meeting point for all of the various components. Because of its importance, the API server deserves deeper introspection and is covered in Chapter 4.

Scheduler

With etcd and the API server operating correctly, a Kubernetes cluster is, in some ways, functionally complete. You can create all of the different API objects, like Deployments and Pods. However, you will find that it never begins to run. Finding a location for a Pod to run is the job of the Kubernetes scheduler. The scheduler scans the API server for unscheduled Pods and then determines the best nodes on which to run them. Like the API server, the scheduler is a complex and rich topic that is covered more deeply in Chapter 5.

Controller manager

After etcd, the API server, and the scheduler are operational, you can successfully create Pods and see them scheduled out onto nodes, but you will find that ReplicaSets, Deployments, and Services don't work as you expect them to. This is because all of the reconciliation control loops needed to implement this functionality are not currently running. Executing these loops is the job of the controller manager. The controller manager is the most varied of all of the Kubernetes components, since it has within it numerous different reconciliation control loops to implement many parts of the overall Kubernetes system.

Components On All Nodes

In addition to the components that run exclusively on the head nodes, there are a few components that are present on all nodes in the Kubernetes cluster. These pieces implement essential functionality that is required on all nodes.

Kubelet

The kubelet is the node daemon for all machines that are part of a Kubernetes cluster. The kubelet is the bridge that joins the available CPU, disk, and memory for a node into the large Kubernetes cluster. The kubelet communicates with the API server to find containers that should be running on its node. Likewise, the kubelet communicates the state of these containers back up to the API server so that other reconciliation control loops can observe the current state of these containers.

In addition to scheduling and reporting the state of containers running in Pods on their machines, kubelets are also responsible for health checking and restarting the containers that are supposed to be executing on their machines. It would be quite inefficient to push all of the health-state information back up to the API server so that reconciliation loops can take action to fix the health of a container on a particular machine. Instead, the kubelet shortcircuits this interaction and runs the reconciliation loop itself. Thus, if a container being run by the kubelet dies or fails its health check, the kubelet restarts it, while also communicating this health state (and the restart) back up to the API server.

kube-proxy

The other component that runs on all machines is the kube-proxy. The kube-proxy is responsible for implementing the Kubernetes Service load-balancer networking model. The kube-proxy is always watching the endpoint objects for all Services in the Kubernetes cluster. The kube-proxy then programs the network on its node so that network requests to the virtual IP address of a Service are, in fact, routed to the endpoints that implement this Service. Every Service in Kubernetes gets a virtual IP address, and the kube-proxy is the daemon responsible for defining and implementing the local load balancer that routes traffic from Pods on the machine to Pods, anywhere in the cluster, that implement the Service.

Scheduled Components

When all of the components just described are successfully operating, they provide a minimally viable Kubernetes cluster. But there are several additional scheduled components that are essential to the Kubernetes cluster that actually rely on the cluster itself for their implementation. This means that, although they are essential to cluster function, they also are scheduled, health checked, operated, and updated using calls to the Kubernetes API server itself.

KubeDNS

The first of these scheduled components is the KubeDNS server. When a Kubernetes Service is created, it gets a virtual IP address, but that IP address is also programmed into a DNS server for easy service discovery. The KubeDNS containers implement this name-service for Kubernetes Service objects. The KubeDNS Service is itself expressed as a Kubernetes Service, so the same routing provided by the kube-proxy routes DNS traffic to the KubeDNS containers. The one important difference is that the KubeDNS service is given a static virtual IP address. This means that the API server can program the DNS server into all of the containers that it creates, implementing the naming and service discovery for Kubernetes services.

In addition to the KubeDNS service that has been present in Kubernetes since the first versions, there is also a newer alternative CoreDNS implementation (*https://coredns.io*) that reached general availability (GA) in the 1.11 release of Kubernetes.

The ability for the DNS service to be swapped out shows both the modularity and the value of using Kubernetes to run components like the DNS server. Replacing KubeDNS with CoreDNS is as easy as stopping one Pod and starting another.

Heapster

The other scheduled component is a binary called Heapster, which is responsible for collecting metrics like CPU, network, and disk usage from all containers running inside the Kubernetes cluster. These metrics can be pushed to a monitoring system, like InfluxDB, for alerting and general monitoring of application health in the cluster. Also, importantly, these metrics are used to implement autoscaling of Pods within the Kubernetes cluster. Kubernetes has an autoscaler implementation, that, for example, can automatically scale the size of a Deployment whenever the CPU usage of the containers in the Deployment goes above 80%. Heapster is the component that collects and aggregates these metrics to power the reconciliation loop implemented by the autoscaler. The autoscaler observes the current state of the world through API calls to Heapster.

As of this writing, Heapster is still the source of metrics for autoscaling in many Kubernetes clusters. However, as of the 1.11 release, it has been deprecated in favor of the new `metrics-server` and Metrics API. Heapster will be removed from Kubernetes in release 1.13.

Add-ons

In addition to these core components, there are numerous systems that you can find on most installations of Kubernetes. These include the Kubernetes dashboard, as well as community add-ons, like functions as a service (FaaS), automatic certificate agents, and many more. There are too many Kubernetes add-ons to describe in a few paragraphs, so extending your Kubernetes cluster is covered in Chapter 13.

Summary

Kubernetes is a somewhat complicated distributed system with a number of different components that implement the complete Kubernetes API, including the control plane nodes, which run the API server, and the etcd cluster, which forms the backing store for the API. Additionally, the scheduler interacts with the API server to schedule containers onto specific worker nodes, and the controller manager operates most of the control loops that keep the cluster functioning correctly. After the cluster is functioning correctly, there are numerous components that run on top of the cluster itself, including the cluster DNS services, the Kubernetes Service load-balancer infrastructure, container monitoring, and more. We explore even more components you can run on your cluster in Chapters 12 and 13.

## CHAPTER 4

The Kubernetes API Server

As mentioned in the overview of the Kubernetes components, the API server is the gateway to the Kubernetes cluster. It is the central touch point that is accessed by all users, automation, and components in the Kubernetes cluster. The API server implements a RESTful API over HTTP, performs all API operations, and is responsible for storing API objects into a persistent storage backend. This chapter covers the details of this operation.

Basic Characteristics for Manageability

For all of its complexity, from the standpoint of management, the Kubernetes API server is actually relatively simple to manage. Because all of the API server's persistent state is stored in a database that is external to the API server, the server itself is state-less and can be replicated to handle request load and for fault tolerance. Typically, in a highly available cluster, the API server is replicated three times.

The API server can be quite chatty in terms of the logs that it outputs. It outputs at least a single line for every request that it receives. Because of this, it is critical that some form of log rolling be added to the API server so that it doesn't consume all available disk space. However, because the API server logs are essential to understanding the operation of the API server, we highly recommend that logs be shipped from the API server to a log aggregation service for subsequent introspection and querying to debug user or component requests to the API.

Pieces of the API Server

Operating the Kubernetes API server involves three core funtions:

API management
  The process by which APIs are exposed and managed by the server

Request processing
  The largest set of functionality that processes individual API requests from a client

Internal control loops
  Internals responsible for background operations necessary to the successful operation of the API server

The following sections cover each of these broad categories.

API Management

Although the primary use for the API is servicing individual client requests, before API requests can be processed, the client must know how to make an API request. Ultimately, the API server is an HTTP server—thus, every API request is an HTTP request. But the characteristics of those HTTP requests must be described so that the client and server know how to communicate. For the purposes of exploration, it's great to have an API server actually up and running so that you can poke at it. You can either use an existing Kubernetes cluster that you have access to, or you can use the minikube tool (*https://github.com/minikube/minikube*) for a local Kubernetes cluster. To make it easy to use the curl tool to explore the API server, run the kubectl tool in proxy mode to expose an unauthenticated API server on localhost:8001 using the following command:

```
kubectl proxy
```

API Paths

Every request to the API server follows a RESTful API pattern where the request is defined by the HTTP path of the request. All Kubernetes requests begin with the prefix /api/ (the core APIs) or /apis/ (APIs grouped by API group). The two different sets of paths are primarily historical. API groups did not originally exist in the Kubernetes API, so the original or "core" objects, like Pods and Services, are maintained under the *'/api/'* prefix without an API group. Subsequent APIs have generally been added under API groups, so they follow the *'/apis/<api-group>/'* path. For example, the Job object is part of the batch API group and is thus found under *'/apis/batch/v1/....*

One additional wrinkle for resource paths is whether the resource is namespaced. Namespaces in Kubernetes add a layer of grouping to objects, namespaced resources can only be created within a namespace, and the name of that namespace is included in the HTTP path for the namespaced resource. Of course, there are resources that do not live in a namespace (the most obvious example is the `Namespace` API object itself) and, in this case, they do not have a namespaces component in their HTTP path.

Here are the components of the two different paths for namespaced resource types:

- */api/v1/namespaces/<namespace-name>/<resource-type-name>/<resource-name>*
- */apis/<api-group>/<api-version>/namespaces/<namespace-name>/<resource-type-name>/<resource-name>*

Here are the components of the two different paths for non-namespaced resource types:

- */api/v1/<resource-type-name>/<resource-name>*
- */apis/<api-group>/<api-version>/<resource-type-name>/<resource-name>*

API Discovery

Of course, to be able to make requests to the API, it is necessary to understand which API objects are available to the client. This process occurs through API discovery on the part of the client. To see this process in action and to explore the API server in a more hands-on manner, we can perform this API discovery ourselves.

First off, to simplify things, we use the `kubectl` command-line tool's built-in `proxy` to provide authentication to our cluster. Run:

```
kubectl proxy
```

This creates a simple server running on port 8001 on your local machine.

We can use this server to start the process of API discovery. We begin by examining the `/api` prefix:

```
$ curl localhost:8001/api
{
  "kind": "APIVersions",
  "versions": [
    "v1"
  ],
  "serverAddressByClientCIDRs": [
    {
      "clientCIDR": "0.0.0.0/0",
      "serverAddress": "10.0.0.1:6443"
    }
  ]
}
```

You can see that the server returned an API object of type `APIVersions`. This object provides us with a `versions` field, which lists the available versions.

In this case, there is just a single one, but for the /apis prefix, there are many. We can use this version to continue our investigation:

```
$ curl localhost:8001/api/v1
{
  "kind": "APIResourceList",
  "groupVersion": "v1",
  "resources": [
    {
....
    {
      "name": "namespaces",
      "singularName": "",
      "namespaced": false,
      "kind": "Namespace",
      "verbs": [
        "create",
        "delete",
        "get",
        "list",
        "patch",
        "update",
        "watch"
      ],
      "shortNames": [
        "ns"
      ]
    },
    ...
    {
      "name": "pods",
      "singularName": "",
      "namespaced": true,
      "kind": "Pod",
      "verbs": [
        "create",
        "delete",
        "deletecollection",
        "get",
        "list",
        "patch",
        "proxy",
        "update",
        "watch"
      ],
      "shortNames": [
        "po"
      ],
      "categories": [
        "all"
      ]
    },
```

```
{
  "name": "pods/attach",
  "singularName": "",
  "namespaced": true,
  "kind": "Pod",
  "verbs": []
},
{
  "name": "pods/binding",
  "singularName": "",
  "namespaced": true,
  "kind": "Binding",
  "verbs": [
    "create"
  ]
},
  ....
]
}
```

(This output is heavily edited for brevity.)

Now we are getting somewhere. We can see that the specific resources available on a certain path are printed out by the API server. In this case, the returned object contains the list of resources exposed under the *api/v1/* path.

The OpenAPI/Swagger JSON specification that describes the API (the meta-API object) contains a variety of interesting information in addition to the resource types. Consider the OpenAPI specification for the Pod object:

```
{
  "name": "pods",
  "singularName": "",
  "namespaced": true,
  "kind": "Pod",
  "verbs": [
    "create",
    "delete",
    "deletecollection",
    "get",
    "list",
    "patch",
    "proxy",
    "update",
    "watch"
  ],
  "shortNames": [
    "po"
  ],
  "categories": [
    "all"
  ]
```

```
    },
    {
      "name": "pods/attach",
      "singularName": "",
      "namespaced": true,
      "kind": "Pod",
      "verbs": []
    }
```

Looking at this object, the `name` field provides the name of this resource. It also indicates the subpath for these resources. Because inferring the pluralization of an English word is challenging, the API resource also contains a `singularName` field, which indicates the name that should be used for a singular instance of this resource. We previously discussed namespaces. The `namespaced` field in the object description indicates whether the object is namespaced. The `kind` field provides the string that is present in the API object's JSON representation to indicate what kind of object it is. The `verbs` field is one of the most important in the API object, because it indicates what kinds of actions can be taken on that object. The `pods` object contains all of the possible verbs. Most of the effects of the verbs are obvious from their names. The two that require a little more explanation are `watch` and `proxy`. `watch` indicates that you can establish a watch for the resource. A watch is a long-running operation that provides notifications about changes to the object. The watch is covered in detail in later sections. `proxy` is a specialized action that establishes a proxy network connection through the API server to network ports. There are only two resources (Pods and Services) that currently support `proxy`.

In addition to the actions (described as verbs) that you can take on an object, there are other actions that are modeled as subresources on a resource type. For example, the `attach` command is modeled as a subresource:

```
    {
      "name": "pods/attach",
      "singularName": "",
      "namespaced": true,
      "kind": "Pod",
      "verbs": []
    }
```

`attach` provides you with the ability to attach a terminal to a running container within a Pod. The `exec` functionality that allows you to execute a command within a Pod is modeled similarly.

OpenAPI Spec Serving

Of course, knowing the resources and paths you can use to access the API server is only part of the information that you need in order to access the Kubernetes API. In addition to the HTTP path, you need to know the JSON payload to send and receive.

The API server also provides paths to supply you with information about the schemas for Kubernetes resources. These schemas are represented using the OpenAPI (formerly Swagger) syntax. You can pull down the OpenAPI specification at the following path:

/swaggerapi
> Before Kubernetes 1.10, serves Swagger 1.2

/openapi/v2
> Kubernetes 1.10 and beyond, serves OpenAPI (Swagger 2.0)

The OpenAPI specification is a complete subject unto itself and is beyond the scope of this book. In any event, it is unlikely that you will need to access it in your day-to-day operations of Kubernetes. However, the various client programming language libraries are generated using these OpenAPI specifications (the notable exception to this is the Go client library, which is currently hand-coded). Thus, if you or a user are having trouble accessing parts of the Kubernetes API via a client library, the first stop should be the OpenAPI specification to understand how the API objects are modeled.

API Translation

In Kubernetes, an API starts out as an alpha API (e.g., v1alpha1). The alpha designation indicates that the API is unstable and unsuitable for production use cases. Users who adopt alpha APIs should expect both that the API surface area may change between Kubernetes releases and that the implementation of the API itself may be unstable and may even destabilize the entire Kubernetes cluster. Alpha APIs are therefore disabled in production Kubernetes clusters.

Once an API has matured, it becomes a beta API (e.g., v1beta1). The beta designation indicates that the API is generally stable but may have bugs or final API surface refinements. In general, beta APIs are assumed to be stable between Kubernetes releases, and backward compatability is a goal. However, in special cases, beta APIs may still be incompatible between Kubernetes releases. Likewise, beta APIs are intended to be stable, but bugs may still exist. Beta APIs are generally enabled in production Kubernetes clusters but should be used carefully.

Finally an API becomes generally available (e.g., v1). General availability (GA) indicates that the API is stable. These APIs come with both a guarantee of backward compatability and a deprecation guarantee. After an API is marked as scheduled for removal, Kubernetes retains the API for at least three releases or one year, whichever comes first. Deprecation is also fairly unlikely. APIs are deprecated only after a superior alternative has been developed. Likewise, GA APIs are stable and suitable for all production usage.

A particular release of Kubernetes can support multiple versions (alpha, beta, and GA). In order to accomplish this, the API server has three different representations of the API at all times: the *external* representation, which is the representation that comes in via an API request; the *internal* representation, which is the in-memory representation of the object used within the API server for processing; and the *storage* representation, which is recorded into the storage layer to persist the API objects. The API server has code within it that knows how to perform the various translations between all of these representations. An API object may be submitted as a `v1alpha1` version, stored as a `v1` object, and subsequently retrieved as a `v1beta1` object or any other arbitrary supported version. These transformations are achieved with reasonable performance using machine-generated *deep-copy* libraries, which perform the appropriate translations.

Request Management

The main purpose of the API server in Kubernetes is to receive and process API calls in the form of HTTP requests. These requests are either from other components in the Kubernetes system or they are end-user requests. In either event, they are all processed by the Kubernetes API server in the same manner.

Types of Requests

There are several broad categories of requests performed by the Kubernetes API server.

GET

> The simplest requests are `GET` requests for specific resources. These requests retrieve the data associated with a particular resource. For example, an HTTP `GET` request to the path */api/v1/namespaces/default/pods/foo* retrieves the data for a Pod named *foo*.

LIST

> A slightly more complicated but still fairly straightforward request is a `collection GET`, or `LIST`. These are requests to list a number of different requests. For example, an HTTP `GET` request to the path */api/v1/namespaces/default/pods* retrieves a collection of all Pods in the `default` namespace. `LIST` requests can also optionally specify a label query, in which case, only resources matching that label query are returned.

POST

> To create a resource, a `POST` request is used. The body of the request is the new resource that should be created. In the case of a `POST` request, the path is the resource type (e.g., */api/v1/namespaces/default/pods*). To update an existing resource, a `PUT` request is made to the specific resource path (e.g., */api/v1/namespaces/default/pods/foo*).

DELETE

When the time comes to delete a request, an HTTP DELETE request to the path of the resource (e.g., */api/v1/namespaces/default/pods/foo*) is used. It's important to note that this change is permanent—after the HTTP request is made, the resource is deleted.

The content type for all of these requests is usually text-based JSON (`application/json`) but recent releases of Kubernetes also support Protocol Buffers binary encoding. Generally speaking, JSON is better for human-readable and debuggable traffic on the network between client and server, but it is significantly more verbose and expensive to parse. Protocol Buffers are harder to introspect using common tools, like `curl`, but enable greater performance and throughput of API requests.

In addition to these standard requests, many requests use the WebSocket protocol to enable streaming sessions between client and server. Examples of such protocols are the `exec` and `attach` commands. These requests are described in the following sections.

Life of a Request

To better understand what the API server is doing for each of these different requests, we'll take apart and describe the processing of a single request to the API server.

Authentication

The first stage of request processing is *authentication*, which establishes the identity associated with the request. The API server supports several different modes of establishing identity, including client certificates, bearer tokens, and HTTP Basic Authentication. In general, client certificates or bearer tokens, should be used for authentication; the use of HTTP Basic Authentication is discouraged.

In addition to these local methods of establishing identity, authentication is pluggable, and there are several plug-in implementations that use remote identity providers. These include support for the OpenID Connect (OIDC) protocol, as well as Azure Active Directory. These authentication plug-ins are compiled into both the API server and the client libraries. This means that you may need to ensure that both the command-line tools and API server are roughly the same version or support the same authentication methods.

The API server also supports remote webhook-based authentication configurations, where the authentication decision is delegated to an outside server via bearer token forwarding. The external server validates the bearer token from the end user and returns the authentication information to the API server.

Given the importance of this in securing a server, it is covered in depth in a later chapter.

RBAC/Authorization

After the API server has determined the identity for a request, it moves on to authorization for it. Every request to Kubernetes follows a traditional RBAC model. To access a request, the identity must have the appropriate role associated with the request. Kubernetes RBAC is a rich and complicated topic, and as such, we have devoted an entire chapter to the details of how it operates. For the purposes of this API server summary, when processing a request, the API server determines whether the identity associated with the request can access the combination of the verb and the HTTP path in the request. If the identity of the request has the appropriate role, it is allowed to proceed. Otherwise, an HTTP 403 response is returned.

This is covered in much more detail in a later chapter.

Admission control

After a request has been authenticated and authorized, it moves on to admission control. Authentication and RBAC determine whether the request is allowed to occur, and this is based on the HTTP properties of the request (headers, method, and path). *Admission control* determines whether the request is well formed and potentially applies modifications to the request before it is processed. Admission control defines a pluggable interface:

```
apply(request): (transformedRequest, error)
```

If any admission controller finds an error, the request is rejected. If the request is accepted, the transformed request is used instead of the initial request. Admission controllers are called serially, each receiving the output of the previous one.

Because admission control is such a general, pluggable mechanism, it is used for a wide variety of different functionality in the API server. For example, it is used to add default values to objects. It can also be used to enforce policy (e.g., requiring that all objects have a certain label). Additionally, it can be used to do things like inject an additional container into every Pod. The service mesh Istio uses this approach to inject its sidecar container transparently.

Admission controllers are quite generic and can be added dynamically to the API server via webhook-based admission control.

Validation

Request validation occurs after admission control, although it can also be implemented as part of admission control, especially for external webhook-based validation. Additionally, validation is only performed on a single object. If it requires broader knowledge of the cluster state, it must be implemented as an admission controller.

Request validation ensures that a specific resource included in a request is valid. For example, it ensures that the name of a `Service` object conforms to the rules around DNS names, since eventually the name of a `Service` will be programmed into the Kubernetes `Service` discovery DNS server. In general, validation is implemented as custom code that is defined per resource type.

Specialized requests

In addition to the standard RESTful requests, the API server has a number of specialized request patterns that provide expanded functionality to clients:

```
/proxy, /exec, /attach, /logs
```

The first important class of operations is open, long-running connections to the API server. These requests provide streaming data rather than immediate responses.

The `logs` operation is the first streaming request we describe, because it is the easiest to understand. Indeed, by default, `logs` isn't a streaming request at all. A client makes a request to get the logs for a Pod by appending `/logs` to the end of the path for a particular Pod (e.g., */api/v1/namespaces/default/pods/some-pod/logs*) and then specifying the container name as an HTTP query parameter and an HTTP `GET` request. Given a default request, the API server returns all of the logs up to the current time, as plain text, and then closes the HTTP request. However, if the client requests that the logs be tailed (by specifying the `follow` query parameter), the HTTP response is kept open by the API server and new logs are written to the HTTP response as they are received from the kubelet via the API server. This connection is shown in Figure 4-1.

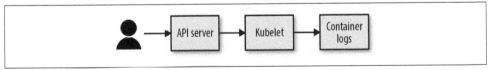

Figure 4-1. The basic flow of an HTTP request for container logs

`logs` is the easiest streaming request to understand because it simply leaves the request open and streams in more data. The rest of the operations take advantage of the WebSocket protocol for bidirectional streaming data. They also actually multiplex data within those streams to enable an arbitrary number of bidirectional streams over HTTP. If this all sounds a little complicated, it is, but it is also a valuable part of the API server's surface area.

> The API server actually supports two different streaming protocols. It supports the SPDY protocol, as well as HTTP2/WebSocket. SPDY is being replaced by HTTP2/WebSocket and thus we focus our attention on the WebSocket protocol.

The full WebSocket protocol is beyond the scope of this book, but it is documented in a number of other places. For the purposes of understanding the API server, you can simply think of WebSocket as a protocol that transforms HTTP into a bidirectional byte-streaming protocol.

However, on top of those streams, the Kubernetes API server actually introduces an additional multiplexed streaming protocol. The reason for this is that, for many use cases, it is quite useful for the API server to be able to service multiple independent byte streams. Consider, for example, executing a command within a container. In this case, there are actually three streams that need to be maintained (stdin, stderr, and stdout).

The basic protocol for this streaming is as follows: every stream is assigned a number from 0 to 255. This stream number is used for both input and output, and it conceptually models a single bidirectional byte stream.

For every frame that is sent via the WebSocket protocol, the first byte is the stream number (e.g., 0) and the remainder of the frame is the data that is traveling on that stream (Figure 4-2).

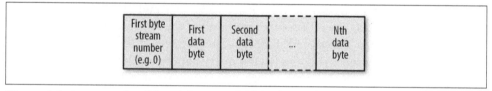

Figure 4-2. An example of the Kubernetes WebSocket multichannel framing

Using this protocol and WebSockets, the API server can simultaneously multiplex 256-byte streams in a single WebSocket session.

This basic protocol is used for exec and attach sessions, with the following channels:

0

The stdin stream for writing to the process. Data is not read from this stream.

1

The stdout output stream for reading stdout from the process. Data should not be written to this stream.

2

The stderr output stream for reading stderr from the process. Data should not be written to this stream.

The /proxy endpoint is used to port-forward network traffic between the client and containers and services running inside the cluster, without those endpoints being externally exposed. To stream these TCP sessions, the protocol is slightly more complicated. In addition to multiplexing the various streams, the first two bytes of the stream (after the stream number, so actually the second and third bytes in the Web-Sockets frame) are the port number that is being forwarded, so that a single Web-Sockets frame for /proxy looks like Figure 4-3.

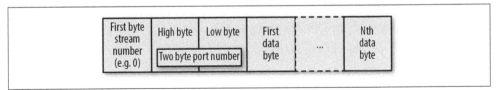

Figure 4-3. An example of the data frame for WebSockets-based port forwarding

Watch operations

In addition to streaming data, the API server supports a watch API. A watch monitors a path for changes. Thus, instead of polling at some interval for possible updates, which introduces either extra load (due to fast polling) or extra latency (because of slow polling), using a watch enables a user to get low-latency updates with a single connection. When a user establishes a watch connection to the API server by adding the query parameter ?watch=true to some API server request, the API server switches into watch mode, and it leaves the connection between client and server open. Likewise, the data returned by the API server is no longer just the API object— it is a Watch object that contains both the type of the change (created, updated, deleted) and the API object itself. In this way, a client can watch and observe all changes to that object or set of objects.

Optimistically concurrent updates

An additional advanced operation supported by the API server is the ability to perform *optimistically concurrent* updates of the Kubernetes API. The idea behind optimistic concurrency is the ability to perform most operations without using locks (*pessimistic concurrency*) and instead detect when a concurrent write has occurred, rejecting the later of the two concurrent writes. A write that is rejected is not retried (it is up to the client to detect the conflict and retry the write themselves).

To understand why this optimistic concurrency and conflict detection is required, it's important to know about the structure of a read/update/write race condition. The operation of many API server clients involves three operations:

1. Read some data from the API server.

2. Update that data in memory.

3. Write it back to the API server.

Now imagine what happens when two of these read/update/write patterns happen simultaneously.

1. Server A reads object O.
2. Server B reads object O.
3. Server A updates object O in memory on the client.
4. Server B updates object O in memory on the client.
5. Server A writes object O.
6. Server B writes object O.

At the end of this, the changes that Server A made are lost because they were overwritten by the update from Server B.

There are two options for solving this race. The first is a pessimistic lock, which would prevent other reads from occurring while Server A is operating on the object. The trouble with this is that it serializes all of the operations, which leads to performance and throughput problems.

The other option implemented by the Kubernetes API server is optimistic concurrency, which assumes that everything will just work out and only detects a problem when a conflicting write is attempted. To achieve this, every instance of an object returns both its data and a resource version. This resource version indicates the current iteration of the object. When a write occurs, if the resource version of the object is set, the write is only successful if the current version matches the version of the object. If it does not, an HTTP error 409 (conflict) is returned and the client musty retry. To see how this fixes the read/update/write race just described, let's take a look at the operations again:

1. Server A reads object O at version v1.
2. Server B reads object O at version v1.
3. Server A updates object O at version v1 in memory in the client.
4. Server B updates object O at version v1 in memory in the client.
5. Server A writes object O at version v1; this is successful.
6. Server B writes object O at version v1, but the object is at v2; a 409 conflict is returned.

Alternate encodings

In addition to supporting JSON encoding of objects for requests, the API server supports two other formats for requests. The encoding of the requests is indicated by the Content-Type HTTP header on the request. If this header is missing, the content is assumed to be `application/json`, which indicates JSON encoding. The first alternate encoding is YAML, which is indicated by the `application/yaml` Content Type. YAML is a text-based format that is generally considered to be more human readable than JSON. There is little reason to use YAML for encoding for communicating with the server, but it can be convenient in a few circumstances (e.g., manually sending files to the server via `curl`).

The other alternate encoding for requests and responses is the Protocol Buffers encoding format. Protocol Buffers are a fairly efficient binary object protocol. Using Protocol Buffers can result in more efficient and higher throughput requests to the API servers. Indeed, many of the Kubernetes internal tools use Protocol Buffers as their transport. The main issue with Protocol Buffers is that, because of their binary nature, they are significantly harder to visualize/debug in their wire format. Additionally, not all client libraries currently support Protocol Buffers requests or responses. The Protocol Buffers format is indicated by the `application/vnd.kubernetes.proto buf` Content-Type header.

Common response codes

Because the API server is implemented as a RESTful server, all of the responses from the server are aligned with HTTP response codes. Beyond the typical 200 for OK responses and 500s for internal server errors, here are some of the common response codes and their meanings:

202
> Accepted. An asyncronous request to create or delete an object has been received. The result responds with a status object until the asynchronous request has completed, at which point the actual object will be returned.

400
> Bad Request. The server could not parse or understand the request.

401
> Unauthorized. A request was received without a known authentication scheme.

403
> Forbidden. The request was received and understood, but access is forbidden.

409
> Conflict. The request was received, but it was a request to update an older version of the object.

422
> Unprocessable entity. The request was parsed correctly but failed some sort of validation.

API Server Internals

In addition to the basics of operating the HTTP RESTful service, the API server has a few internal services that implement parts of the Kubernetes API. Generally, these sorts of control loops are run in a separate binary known as the controller manager. But there are a few control loops that have to be run inside the API server. In each case, we describe the functionality as well as the reason for its presence in the API server.

CRD Control Loop

Custom resource definitions (CRDs) are dynamic API objects that can be added to a running API server. Because the act of creating a CRD inherently creates new HTTP paths the API server must know how to serve, the controller that is responsible for adding these paths is colocated inside the API server. With the addition of delegated API servers (described in a later chapter), this controller has actually been mostly abstracted out of the API server. It currently still runs in process by default, but it can also be run out of process.

The CRD control loop operates as follows:

```
for crd in AllCustomResourceDefinitions:
    if !RegisteredPath(crd):
        registerPath

for path in AllRegisteredPaths:
    if !CustomResourceExists(path):
        markPathInvalid(path)
        delete custom resource data
        delete path
```

The creation of the custom resource path is fairly straightforward, but the deletion of a custom resource is a little more complicated. This is because the deletion of a custom resource implies the deletion of all data associated with resources of that type. This is so that, if a CRD is deleted and then at some later date readded, the old data does not somehow get resurrected.

Thus, before the HTTP serving path can be removed, the path is first marked as invalid so that new resources cannot be created. Then, all data associated with the CRD is deleted, and finally, the path is removed.

Debugging the API Server

Of course, understanding the implementation of the API server is great, but more often than not, what you really need is to be able to debug what is actually going on with the API server (as well as clients that are calling in to the API server). The primary way that this is achieved is via the logs that the API server writes. There are two log streams that the API server exports—the *standard* or *basic* logs, as well as the more targeted *audit* logs that try to capture why and how requests were made and the changed API server state. In addition, more verbose logging can be turned on for debugging specific problems.

Basic Logs

By default, the API server logs every request that is sent to the API server. This log includes the client's IP address, the path of the request, and the code that the server returned. If an unexpected error results in a server panic, the server also catches this panic, returns a 500, and logs that error.

```
I0803 19:59:19.929302        1 trace.go:76] Trace[1449222206]:
"Create /api/v1/namespaces/default/events" (started: 2018-08-03
19:59:19.001777279 +0000 UTC m=+25.386403121) (total time: 927.484579ms):
Trace[1449222206]: [927.401927ms] [927.279642ms] Object stored in database
I0803 19:59:20.402215        1 controller.go:537] quota admission added
evaluator for: { namespaces}
```

In this log, you can see that it starts with the timestamp I0803 19:59:… when the log line was emitted, followed by the line number that emitted it, trace.go:76, and finally the log message itself.

Audit Logs

The *audit log* is intended to enable a server administrator to forensically recover the state of the server and the series of client interactions that resulted in the current state of the data in the Kubernetes API. For example, it enables a user to answer questions like, "Why was that ReplicaSet scaled up to 100?", "Who deleted that Pod?", among others.

Audit logs have a pluggable backend for where they are written. Generally, audit logs are written to file, but it is also possible for them to be written to a webhook. In either case, the data logged is a structured JSON object of type event in the audit.k8s.io API group.

Auditing itself can be configured via a policy object in the same API group. This policy allows you to specify the rules by which audit events are emitted into the audit log.

Activating Additional Logs

Kubernetes uses the github.com/golang/glog leveled logging package for its logging. Using the --v flag on the API server you can adjust the level of logging verbosity. In general, the Kubernetes project has set log verbosity level 2 (--v=2) as a sane default for logging relevant, but not too spammy messages. If you are looking into specific problems, you can raise the logging level to see more (possibly spammy) messages.

Because of the performance impact of excessive logging, we recommend not running with a verbose log level in production. If you are looking for more targeted logging, the --vmodule flag enables increasing the log level for individual source files. This can be useful for very targeted verbose logging restricted to a small set of files.

Debugging kubectl Requests

In addition to debugging the API server via logs, it is also possible to debug interactions with the API server, via the kubectl command-line tool. Like the API server, the kubectl command-line tool logs via the github.com/golang/glog package and supports the --v verbosity flag. Setting the verbosity to level 10 (--v=10) turns on maximally verbose logging. In this mode, kubectl logs all of the requests that it makes to the server, as well as attempts to print curl commands that you can use to replicate these requests. Note that these curl commands are sometimes incomplete.

Additionally, if you want to poke at the API server directly, the approach that we used earlier to explore API discovery works well. Running kubectl proxy creates a proxy server on localhost that automatically supplies your authentication and authorization credentials, based on a local *$HOME/.kube/config* file. After you run the proxy, it's fairly straightforward to poke at various API requests using the curl command.

Summary

As an operator, the core service that you are providing to your users is the Kubernetes API. To effectively provide this service, understanding the core components that make up Kubernetes and how your users will put these APIs together to build applications is critical to implementing a useful and reliable Kubernetes cluster. Having finished reading this chapter, you should have a basic knowledge of the Kubernetes API and how it is used.

## CHAPTER 5

Scheduler

One of the primary jobs of the Kubernetes API is to schedule containers to worker nodes in the cluster of machines. This task is accomplished by a dedicated binary in the Kubernetes cluster called the Kubernetes scheduler. This chapter describes how the scheduler operates, how it can be extended, and how it can even be replaced or augmented by additional schedulers. Kubernetes can handle a wide variety of workloads, from stateless web serving to stateful applications, big data batch jobs, or machine learning on GPUs. The key to ensuring that all of these very different applications can operate in harmony on the same cluster lies in the application of *job scheduling*, which ensures that each container is placed onto the worker node best suited to it.

An Overview of Scheduling

When a Pod is first created, it generally doesn't have a nodeName field. The nodeName indicates the node on which the Pod should execute. The Kubernetes scheduler is constantly scanning the API server (via a watch request) for Pods that don't have a nodeName; these are Pods that are eligible for scheduling. The scheduler then selects an appropriate node for the Pod and updates the Pod definition with the nodeName that the scheduler selected. After the nodeName is set, the kubelet running on that node is notified about the Pod's existence (again, via a watch request) and it begins to actually execute that Pod on that node.

If you want to skip the scheduler, you can always set the `nodeName` yourself on a Pod. This direct schedules a Pod onto a specific node. This is, in fact, how the `DaemonSet` controller schedules a single Pod onto each node in the cluster. In general, however, direct scheduling should be avoided, since it tends to make your application more brittle and your cluster less efficient. In the general use case, you should trust the scheduler to make the right decision, just as you trust the operating system to find a core to execute your program when you launch it on a single machine.

Scheduling Process

When the scheduler discovers a Pod that hasn't been assigned to a node, it needs to determine which node to schedule the Pod onto. The correct node for a Pod is determined by a number of different factors, some of which are supplied by the user and some of which are calculated by the scheduler. In general, the scheduler is trying to optimize a variety of different criteria to find the node that is best for the particular Pod.

Predicates

When making the decision about how to schedule a Pod, the scheduler uses two generic concepts to make its decision. The first is *predicates*. Simply stated, a predicate indicates whether a Pod fits onto a particular node. Predicates are hard constraints, which, if violated, lead to a Pod not operating correctly (or at all) on that node. An example of a such a constraint is the amount of memory requested by the Pod. If that memory is unavailable on the node, the Pod cannot get all of the memory that it needs and the constraint is violated—it is false. Another example of a predicate is a node-selector label query specified by the user. In this case, the user has requested that a Pod only run on certain machines as indicated by the node labels. The predicate is false if a node does not have the required label.

Priorities

Predicates indicate situations that are either true or false—the Pod either fits or it doesn't—but there is an additional generic interface used by the scheduler to determine preference for one node over another. These preferences are expressed as *priorities* or *priority functions*. The role of a priority function is to score the relative value of scheduling a Pod onto a particular node. In contrast to predicates, the priority function does not indicate whether or not the Pod being scheduled onto the node is viable—it is assumed that the Pod can successfully execute on the node—but instead, the predicate function attempts to judge the relative value of scheduling the Pod onto that particular node.

As an example, a priority function would weight nodes where the image has already been pulled. Therefore, the container would start faster than nodes where the image is not present and would have to be pulled, delaying Pod startup.

One important priority function is the spreading function. This function is responsible for prioritizing nodes where Pods that are members of the same Kubernetes Service are not present. It is used to ensure reliability, since it reduces the chances that a machine failure will disable all of the containers in a particular Service.

Ultimately, all of the various predicate values are mixed together to achieve a final priority score for the node, and this score is used to determine where the Pod is scheduled.

High-Level Algorithm

For every Pod that needs scheduling, the scheduling algorithm is run. At a high level, the algorithm looks like this:

```
schedule(pod): string
    nodes := getAllHealthyNodes()
    viableNodes := []
    for node in nodes:
        for predicate in predicates:
            if predicate(node, pod):
                viableNodes.append(node)

    scoredNodes := PriorityQueue<score, Node[]>
    priorities := GetPriorityFunctions()
    for node in viableNodes:
        score = CalculateCombinedPriority(node, pod, priorities)
        scoredNodes[score].push(node)

    bestScore := scoredNodes.top().score
    selectedNodes := []
    while scoredNodes.top().score == bestScore:
      selectedNodes.append(scoredNodes.pop())

    node := selectAtRandom(selectedNodes)
    return node.Name
```

You can find the actual code on the Kubernetes GitHub page (*http://bit.ly/2Or3Y5Z*).

The basic operation of the scheduler is as follows: first, the scheduler gets the list of all currently known and healthy nodes. Then, for each predicate, the scheduler evaluates the predicate against the node and the Pod being scheduled. If the node is viable (the Pod could run on it), the node is added to the list of possible nodes for scheduling. Next, all of the priority functions are run against the combination of Pod and node. The results are pushed into a priority queue ordered by score, with the best-scoring nodes at the top of the queue. Then, all nodes that have the same score are popped off of the priority queue and placed into a final list. They are considered to be entirely identical, and one of them is chosen in a round-robin fashion and is then returned as the node where the Pod should be scheduled. Round robin is used instead of random choice to ensure an even distribution of Pods among identical nodes.

Conflicts

Because there is lag time between when a Pod is scheduled (time T_1) and when the container actually executes (time T_N), the scheduling decision may become invalid, due to other actions during the time interval between scheduling and execution.

In some cases, this may mean that a slightly less ideal node is chosen, when a better one could have been assigned. This could be caused by a Pod terminating after time T_1 but before time T_N or other changes to the cluster. In general, these sorts of soft-constraint conflicts aren't that important and they normalize in the aggregate. These conflicts are thus ignored by Kubernetes. Scheduling decisions are only optimal for a single moment in time—they can always become worse as time passes and the cluster changes.

 There is some work going on in the Kubernetes community to improve this situation somewhat. A Kubernetes-descheduler project (*https://github.com/kubernetes-incubator/descheduler*), which, if run in a Kubernetes cluster, scans it for Pods that are determined to be significantly suboptimal. If such Pods are found, the descheduler evicts the Pod from its current node. Consequently, the Pod is rescheduled by the Kubernetes scheduler, as if it had just been created.

A more significant kind of conflict occurs when a change to the cluster violates a hard constraint of the scheduler. Imagine, for example, that the scheduler decides to place Pod P on node N. Imagine that Pod P requires two cores to operate, and node N has exactly two cores of spare capacity. At time T_1, the scheduler has determined that node N has sufficient capacity to run Pod P. However, after the scheduler makes its decision in code and before the decision is written back to the Pod, a new DaemonSet is created. This DaemonSet creates a different Pod that runs on every node, including node N, which consumes one core of capacity. Now Node N only has a single core free, and yet it has been asked to run Pod P, which requires two cores. This is not possible, given the new state of node N, but the scheduling decision has already been made.

When the node notices that it has been asked to run a Pod that no longer passes the predicates for the Pod and node, the Pod is marked as failed. If the Pod has been created by a ReplicaSet, this failed Pod doesn't count as an active member of the ReplicaSet and, thus, a new Pod will be created and scheduled onto a different node where it fits. This failure behavior is important to understand because it means that Kubernetes cannot be counted on to reliably run standalone Pods. You should always run Pods (even singletons) via a `ReplicaSet` or Deployment.

Controlling Scheduling with Labels, Affinity, Taints, and Tolerations

Of course, there are times when you want more fine-grained control of the scheduling decisions that Kubernetes performs. You could have this by adding your own predicates and priorities, but that's a fairly heavyweight task. Fortunately, Kubernetes provides you with a number of tools to customize scheduling—without having to implement anything in your own code.

Node Selectors

Remember that every object in Kubernetes has an associated set of *labels*. Labels provide identifying metadata for Kubernetes objects, and *label selectors* are often used to dynamically identify sets of API objects for various operations. For example, labels and label selectors are used to identify the sets of Pods that serve traffic behind a Kubernetes load balancers.

Label selectors can also be used to identify a subset of the nodes in a Kubernetes cluster that should be used for scheduling a particular Pod. By default, all nodes in the cluster are potential candidates for scheduling, but by filling in the `spec.nodeSelec tor` field in a Pod or PodTemplate, the initial set of nodes can be reduced to a subset.

As an example, consider the task of scheduling a workload to a machine that has high-performance storage, like NVMe-backed SSD. Such storage (at least at the time of this writing) is very expensive and therefore may not be present in every machine. Thus, every machine that has this storage will be given an extra label like:

```
kind: Node
metadata:
  - labels:
      nvme-ssd: true
  ...
```

To create a Pod that will always be scheduled onto a machine with an NVMe SSD, you then set the Pod's `nodeSelector` to match the label on the node:

```
kind: Pod
spec:
  nodeSelector:
    nvme-ssd: true
  ...
```

Kubernetes has a default predicate that requires every node to match the nodeSelec
tor label query, if it is present. Thus, every Pod with the nvme-ssd label will always be
scheduled onto a node with the appropriate hardware.

As was mentioned earlier in the section on conflicts, Node selectors are only evaluated at the time of scheduling. If nodes are actively added and removed, by the time
the container executes, its node selector may no longer match the node where it is
running.

Node Affinity

Node selectors provide a simple way to guarantee that a Pod lands on a particular
node, but they lack flexibility. In particular, they cannot represent more complex logical expressions (e.g., "Label foo is either A or B.") nor can they represent *antiaffinity*
("Label foo is A but label bar is not C."). Finally, node selectors are predicates—they
specify a requirement, not a preference.

Starting with Kubernetes 1.2, the notion of *affinity* was added to node selection via
the affinity structure in the Pod spec. Affinity is a more complicated structure to
understand, but it is significantly more flexible if you want to express more complicated scheduling policies.

Consider the example just noted, in which a Pod should schedule onto a node that
has either label foo has a value of either A or B. This is expressed as the following
affinity policy:

```
kind: Pod
...
spec:
  affinity:
    nodeAffinity:
      requiredDuringSchedulingIgnoredDuringExecution:
        nodeSelectorTerms:
        - matchExpressions:
          # foo == A or B
          - key: foo
            operator: In
            values:
            - A
            - B
...
```

To show antiaffinity, consider the policy label foo has value A and label bar does not
equal C. This is expressed in a similar, though slightly more complicated, specification:

```
kind: Pod
...
spec:
```

```
  affinity:
    nodeAffinity:
      requiredDuringSchedulingIgnoredDuringExecution:
        nodeSelectorTerms:
        - matchExpressions:
          # foo == A
          - key: foo
            operator: In
            values:
            - A
          # bar != C
          - key: bar
            operator: NotIn
            values:
            - C
...
```

> These two examples include the operators In and NotIn. Kubernetes also allows Exists, which only requires that a label key be present regardless of value, as well as NotExists, which requires that a label be absent. There are also Gt and Lt operators, which implement greater-than and less-than, respectively. If you use the Gt or Lt operators, the values array is expected to consist of a single integer and your node labels are expected to be integrals.

So far, we've seen node affinity provide a more sophisticated way to select nodes, but we have still only expressed a predicate. This is due to requiredDuringSchedulingIgnoredDuringExecution, which is a long-winded but accurate description of the node affinity behavior. The label expression must match when scheduling is performed but may not match when the Pod is executing.

If you want to express a priority for a node instead of a requirement (or in addition to a requirement), you can use preferredDuringSchedulingIgnoredDuringExecution. For example, using our earlier example, where we required that foo be either A or B, let's also express a preference for scheduling onto nodes labeled A. The weight term in the preference struct allows us to tune how significant a preference it is, relative to other priorities.

```
kind: Pod
...
spec:
  affinity:
    nodeAffinity:
      requiredDuringSchedulingIgnoredDuringExecution:
        nodeSelectorTerms:
        - matchExpressions:
          # foo == A or B
          - key: foo
```

```
      operator: In
      values:
      - A
      - B
  preferredDuringSchedulingIgnoredDuringExecution:
    preference:
  - weight: 1
    matchExpressions:
    # foo == A
    - key: foo
      operator: In
      values:
      - A
...
```

Node affinity is currently a beta feature. In Kubernetes 1.4 and beyond, Pod affinity was also introduced with similar syntax (substituting pod for node). Pod affinity allows you to express a requirement or preference for scheduling alongside—or away from—other Pods with particular labels.

Taints and Tolerations

Node and Pod affinity allow you to specify preferences for a Pod to schedule (or not) onto a specific set of nodes or near a specific set of Pods. However, that requires user action when creating containers to achieve the right scheduling behavior. Sometimes, as the administrator of a cluster, you might want to affect scheduling without requiring your users to change their behavior.

For example, consider a heterogenous Kubernetes cluster. You may have a mixture of hardware types—some with old 1 Ghz processors and some with new 3 Ghz processors. In general, you don't want your users to have their work scheduled onto the older processors unless specifically requested. You can achieve this with node antiaffinity, since it requires that every user explicitly add antiaffinity to their Pods for the older machines.

It is this use case that motivated the development of *node taints*. A node taint is exactly what it sounds like. When a taint is applied to a node, the node is considered tainted and will be excluded by default from scheduling. Any tainted node will fail a predicate check at the time of scheduling.

However, consider a user who wants to access 1 Ghz machines. Their work isn't time critical, and the 1 Ghz machines cost less, since there is far less demand. To achieve this, the user opts into the 1 Ghz machines by adding a *toleration* for the particular taint. This toleration enables the scheduling predicate to pass and thus allows for the node to schedule onto the tainted machine. It is important to note that, although a toleration for a taint enables a Pod to run on a tainted machine, it does not require that the Pod runs on the tainted machine. Indeed, all of the priorities run just as before and, thus, all of the machines in the cluster are available to execute on. Forcing a Pod onto a particular machine is a use case for `nodeSelectors` or affinity as described earlier.

Summary

One of the core features of Kubernetes is the ability to take a user's request to execute a container and schedule that container onto an appropriate machine. For a cluster administrator, the operation of the scheduler—and teaching users how to use it well —can be critical to building a cluster that is reliable and that you can drive to high utilization and efficiency.

## CHAPTER 6

Installing Kubernetes

To fully conceptualize and understand how Kubernetes works, it is imperative to experiment with an actual Kubernetes cluster. And, fortunately, there is no shortage of tools to get going with Kubernetes—typically, this can be achieved within a matter of minutes. Whether it be a local installation on your laptop with a tool like minikube (*https://github.com/kubernetes/minikube*) or a managed deployment from any one of the major public cloud providers, a Kubernetes cluster can be had by just about anyone.

Although many of these projects and services have greatly helped to commoditize the deployment of a cluster, there are many circumstances that do not allow for this degree of flexibility. Perhaps there are internal compliance or regulatory constraints that prevent the use of a public cloud. Or maybe your organization has already invested heavily in their own datacenters. Whatever the circumstances, you will be hard pressed to find an environment that is not suitable for a Kubernetes deployment.

Beyond the logistics of where and how you consume Kubernetes, in order to fully appreciate how the distributed components of Kubernetes operate, it is also important to understand the architectures that make production-ready, containerized application delivery a reality. In this chapter, we explore the services involved and how they are installed.

kubeadm

Among the wide array of Kubernetes installation solutions is the community-supported kubeadm utility. This application provides all of the functionality needed to install Kubernetes. In fact, in the simplest of cases, a user can have a Kubernetes installation operational in a matter of minutes—with just a single command. This simplicity makes it a very compelling tool for developers and for those with production-grade needs. Because the code for kubeadm lives in-tree and is released in conjunction with a Kubernetes release, it borrows common primitives and is thoroughly tested for a large number of use cases.

Because of the simplicity and great utility provided by kubeadm, many other installation tools actually leverage kubeadm behind the scenes. And the number of projects following this trend increases regularly. So, regardless of whether you ultimately choose kubeadm as your preferred installation tool, understanding how it works will likely help you further understand the tool you have chosen.

A production-grade deployment of Kubernetes ensures that data is secured, both during transport and at rest, that the Kubernetes components are well matched with their dependencies, that integrations with the environment are well defined, and that the configuration of all the cluster components work well together. Ideally, too, these clusters are easily upgraded and the resulting configuration is continually reflective of these best practices. kubeadm can help you achieve all of this.

Requirements

kubeadm, just like all of the Kubernetes binaries, is statically linked. As such, there are no dependencies on any shared libraries, and kubeadm may be installed on just about any x86_64, ARM, or PowerPC Linux distribution.

Fortunately, there is also not much that we need from a host application perspective, either. Most fundamentally, we require a container runtime and the Kubernetes kubelet, but there are also a few necessary standard Linux utilities.

When it comes to installing a container runtime, you should ensure that it adheres to the Container Runtime Interface (CRI). This open standard defines the interface that the kubelet uses to speak to the runtime available on the host. At the time of this writing, some of the most popular CRI-compliant runtimes are Docker, rkt, and CRI-O. For each of these, developers should consult the installation instructions provided by the respective projects.

When choosing a container runtime, be sure to reference the Kubernetes release notes. Each release will clearly indicate which container runtimes have been tested. This way you know which runtimes and versions are known to be both compatible and performant.

kubelet

As you may recall from Chapter 3, the kubelet is the on-host process responsible for interfacing with the container runtime. In the most common cases, this work typically amounts to reporting node status to the API server and managing the full lifecycle of Pods that have been scheduled to the host on which it resides.

Installation of the kubelet is usually as simple as downloading and installing the appropriate package for the target distribution. In all cases, you should be sure to install the kubelet with a version that matches the Kubernetes version you intend to run. The kubelet is the single Kubernetes process that is managed by the host service manager. In almost all cases, this is likely to be `systemd`.

If you are installing the kubelet with the system packages built and provided by the community (currently `deb` and `rpm`), the kubelet will be managed by *systemd*. As with any process managed in this way, a unit file defines which user the service runs as, what the command-line options are, how the service dependency chain is defined, and what the restart policy should be:

```
[Unit]
Description=kubelet: The Kubernetes Node Agent
Documentation=http://kubernetes.io/docs/

[Service]
ExecStart=/usr/bin/kubelet
Restart=always
StartLimitInterval=0
RestartSec=10

[Install]
WantedBy=multi-user.target
```

Even if you are not installing the kubelet with the community-provided packages, examining the provided unit files is often be helpful for understanding common best practices for running the kubelet daemon. These unit files change often, so be sure to reference the versions that match your deployment target.

The behavior of the kubelet can be manipulated by adding additional unit files to the */etc/systemd/system/kubelet.service.d/* path. These unit files are read lexically (so name them appropriately) and allow you to override how the package configures the kubelet. This may be required if your environment calls for specific needs (i.e., container registry proxies).

For example, when deploying Kubernetes to a supported cloud provider, you need to set the `--cloud-provider` parameter on the kubelet:

```
$ cat /etc/systemd/system/kubelet.service.d/09-extra-args.conf
[Service]
Environment="KUBELET_EXTRA_ARGS= --cloud-provider=aws"
```

With this additional file in place, we simply perform a daemon reload and then restart the service:

```
$ sudo systemctl daemon-reload
$ sudo systemctl restart kubelet
```

By and large, the default configurations provided by the community are typically more than adequate and usually do not require modification. With this technique, however, we can utilize the community defaults while simultaneously maintaining our ability to override, when applicable.

The kubelet and container runtime are necessary on all hosts in the cluster.

Installing the Control Plane

Within Kubernetes the componentry that directs the actions of the worker nodes is termed the control plane. As we covered in Chapter 3, these components consist of the API server, the controller manager, and the scheduler. Each of these daemons directs some portion of how the cluster ultimately operates.

In addition to the Kubernetes components, we require a place to store our cluster state. That data store is etcd.

Fortunately, kubeadm is capable of installing all of these daemons on a host (or hosts) that we, as administrators, have delegated as a control plane node. kubeadm does so by creating a static manifest for each of the daemons that we require.

 With static manifests, we can write Pod specifications directly to disk, and the kubelet, upon start, immediately attempts to launch the containers specified therein. In fact, the kubelet also monitors these files for changes and attempts to reconcile any specified changes. Note, however, that since these Pods are not managed by the control plane, they cannot be manipulated with the kubectl command-line interface.

In addition to the daemons, we need to secure the components with Transport Layer Security (TLS), create a user that can interact with the API, and provide the capability for worker nodes to join the cluster. Kubeadm does all of this.

In the simplest of scenarios, we can install the control plane components on a node that has already been prepared with a running kubelet and functional container runtime, like so:

```
$ kubeadm init
```

After detailed descriptions of the steps kubeadm has taken on behalf of the user, the end of the output might look something like this:

```
...
Your Kubernetes master has initialized successfully!

To start using your cluster, you need to run the following as a regular user:

  mkdir -p $HOME/.kube
  sudo cp -i /etc/kubernetes/admin.conf $HOME/.kube/config
  sudo chown $(id -u):$(id -g) $HOME/.kube/config

You should now deploy a pod network to the cluster.
Run "kubectl apply -f [podnetwork].yaml" with one of the options listed at:
  https://kubernetes.io/docs/concepts/cluster-administration/addons/

You can now join any number of machines by running the following on each node
as root:

  kubeadm join --token 878b76.ddab3219269370b2 10.1.2.15:6443 \
    --discovery-token-ca-cert-hash \
    sha256:312ce807a9e98d544f5a53b36ae3bb95cdcbe50cf8d1294d22ab5521ddb54d68
```

kubeadm Configuration

Although kubeadm init is the simplest case for configuring a controller node, kubeadm is capable of managing all sorts of configurations. This can be achieved by way of the various but somewhat limited number of kubeadm command-line flags, as well as the more capable kubeadm API.

The API looks something like this:

```
apiVersion: kubeadm.k8s.io/v1alpha1
kind: MasterConfiguration
api:
  advertiseAddress: <address|string>
  bindPort: <int>
etcd:
  endpoints:
  - <endpoint1|string>
  - <endpoint2|string>
  caFile: <path|string>
  certFile: <path|string>
  keyFile: <path|string>
networking:
  dnsDomain: <string>
  serviceSubnet: <cidr>
  podSubnet: <cidr>
kubernetesVersion: <string>
cloudProvider: <string>
authorizationModes:
- <authorizationMode1|string>
```

```
- <authorizationMode2|string>
token: <string>
tokenTTL: <time duration>
selfHosted: <bool>
apiServerExtraArgs:
  <argument>: <value|string>
  <argument>: <value|string>
controllerManagerExtraArgs:
  <argument>: <value|string>
  <argument>: <value|string>
schedulerExtraArgs:
  <argument>: <value|string>
  <argument>: <value|string>
apiServerCertSANs:
- <name1|string>
- <name2|string>
certificatesDir: <string>
```

It may be provided to the kubeadm command line with the `--config` flag. Regardless of whether you, as an administrator, decide to explicitly use this configuration format, one is always generated internally upon executing kubeadm `init`. Moreover, this configuration is saved as a `ConfigMap` to the just-provisioned cluster. This functionality serves two purposes—first, to provide a reference for those who need to understand how a cluster was configured, and second, it may be leveraged when upgrading a cluster. In the event of upgrading a cluster, a user modifies the values of this `Config Map` and then executes a kubeadm `upgrade`.

The kubeadm configuration is also accessible by standard kubectl `ConfigMap` interrogation and is, by convention, named the `cluster-info` ConfigMap in the `kube-public` namespace.

Preflight Checks

After we have run this command, kubeadm first executes a number of preflight checks. These sanity checks ensure that our system is appropriate for an install. "Is the kubelet running?", "Has swap been disabled?", and "Are baseline system utilities installed?" are the types of questions that are asked here. And, naturally, kubeadm exits with an error if these baseline conditions are not met.

Although not recommended, it is possible to sidestep the preflight checks with the `--skip-preflight-checks` command-line option. This should only be exercised by advanced administrators.

Certificates

After all preflight checks have been satisfied, kubeadm, by default, generates its own certificate authority (CA) and key. This CA is then used to, subsequently, sign various certificates against it. Some of these certificates are used by the API server when securing inbound requests, authenticating users, making outbound requests (i.e., to an aggregate API server), and for mutual TLS between the API server and all downstream kubelets. Others are used to secure service accounts.

All of these public key infrastructure (PKI) assets are placed in the */etc/kubernetes/pki* directory on the control plane node:

```
$ ls -al /etc/kubernetes/pki/
total 56
drwxr-xr-x 2 root root 4096 Mar 15 02:42 .
drwxr-xr-x 4 root root 4096 Mar 15 02:42 ..
-rw-r--r-- 1 root root 1229 Mar 15 02:42 apiserver.crt
-rw------- 1 root root 1675 Mar 15 02:42 apiserver.key
-rw-r--r-- 1 root root 1099 Mar 15 02:42 apiserver-kubelet-client.crt
-rw------- 1 root root 1679 Mar 15 02:42 apiserver-kubelet-client.key
-rw-r--r-- 1 root root 1025 Mar 15 02:42 ca.crt
-rw------- 1 root root 1675 Mar 15 02:42 ca.key
-rw-r--r-- 1 root root 1025 Mar 15 02:42 front-proxy-ca.crt
-rw------- 1 root root 1675 Mar 15 02:42 front-proxy-ca.key
-rw-r--r-- 1 root root 1050 Mar 15 02:42 front-proxy-client.crt
-rw------- 1 root root 1675 Mar 15 02:42 front-proxy-client.key
-rw------- 1 root root 1675 Mar 15 02:42 sa.key
-rw------- 1 root root  451 Mar 15 02:42 sa.pub
```

> Since this default CA is self-signed, any third-party consumers need to also provide the CA certificate chain when attempting to use a client certificate. Fortunately, this is not typically problematic for Kubernetes users, since a kubeconfig file is capable of embedding this data, and is done automatically by kubeadm.

Self-signed certificates, although extremely convenient, are sometimes not the preferred approach. This is often especially true in corporate environments or for those with more exacting compliance requirements. In this case, a user may prepopulate these assets in the */etc/kubernetes/pki* directory prior to executing kubeadm init. In this case, kubeadm attempts to use the keys and certificates that may already be in place and to generate those that may not already be present.

etcd

In addition to the Kubernetes components that are configured by way of kubeadm, by default, if not otherwise specified, kubeadm attempts to start a local etcd server instance. This daemon is started in the same manner as the Kubernetes components (static manifests) and persists its data to the control plane node's filesystem via local host volume mounts.

> At the time of this writing, `kubeadm init`, by itself, does not natively secure the kubeadm-managed etcd server with TLS. This basic command is only intended to configure a single control plane node and, is typically, for development purposes only.
>
> Users that need kubeadm for production installs should provide a list of TLS-secured etcd endpoints with the `--config` option described earlier in this chapter.

Although having an easily deployable etcd instance is favorable for a simple Kubernetes installation process, it is not appropriate for a production-grade deployment. In a production-grade deployment, an administrator deploys a multinode and highly available etcd cluster that sits adjacent to the Kubernetes deployment. Since the etcd data store will contain all states for the cluster, it is important to treat it with care. Although Kubernetes components are easily replaceable, etcd is not. And, as a result, etcd has a component life cycle (install, upgrade, maintenance, etc.) that is quite different. For this reason, a production Kubernetes cluster should segregate these responsibilities.

Secrets data

All data that is written to etcd is unencrypted by default. If someone were to gain privileged access to the disk backing etcd, the data would be readily available. Fortunately, much of the data that Kubernetes persists to disk is not sensitive in nature.

The exception, however, is Secret data. As the name suggests, Secret data should remain, secret. To ensure that this data is encrypted on its way to etcd, administrators ought to the `--experimental-encryption-provider-config` `kube-apiserver` parameter. With this parameter, administrators can define symmetric keys to encrypt all Secret data.

> At the time of this writing, `--experimental-encryption-provider-config` is still an experimental kube-apiserver command-line parameter. Since this is subject to change, native support for this feature in kubeadm is limited. You may still make use of this feature by adding `encryption.conf` to the */etc/kubernetes/pki* directory of all control plane nodes and by adding this configuration parameter to the `apiServerExtraArgs` field within your kubeadm MasterConfig prior to `kubeadm init`.

This is accomplished with an `EncryptionConfig`:

```
$ cat encryption.conf
kind: EncryptionConfig
apiVersion: v1
resources:
  - resources:
    - secrets
    providers:
    - identity: {}
    - aescbc:
        keys:
        - name: encryptionkey
          secret: BHk4lSZnaMjPYtEHR/jRmLp+ymazbHirgxBHoJZqU/Y=
```

For the recommended `aescbc` encryption type, the `secret` field should be a randomly generated 32-byte key. Now, by adding `--experimental-encryption-provider-config=/path/to/encryption.conf` to the `kube-apiserver` command-line parameters, all Secrets are encrypted before being written to etcd. This may help prevent the leakage of sensitive data.

You may have noticed that the `EncryptionConfig` also includes a `resources` field. For our use case, Secrets are the only resources we want to encrypt, but any resource type may be included here. Use this according to your organization's needs, but remember that encrypting this data does marginally impact performance of the API server's writes. As a general rule of thumb, only encrypt the data that you deem sensitive.

This configuration supports multiple encryption types, some of which may be more or less appropriate for your specific needs. Likewise, this configuration also supports key rotation, a measure that is necessary to ensure a strong security stance. Be sure to consult the Kubernetes documentation for additional details on this experimental feature.

Your requirements for data at rest will have dependencies on your architecture. If you have chosen to colocate your etcd instances on your control plane nodes, utilizing this feature might not serve your needs, since encryption keys would also be colocated with the data. In the event that privileged access to the disk is gained, the keys may be used to unencrypt the etcd data, thus subverting efforts to secure these resources. This is yet another compelling reason for segregating etcd from your Kubernetes control plane nodes.

kubeconfig

In addition to creating the PKI assets and configuring the static manifests that serve the Kubernetes components, kubeadm also generates a number of *kubeconfig* files.

Each of these files will be used for some means of authentication. Most of these will be used to authenticate each of the Kubernetes services against the API, but kubeadm also creates a primary administrator *kubeconfig* file at */etc/kubernetes/admin.conf*.

> Because kubeadm so easily creates this *kubeconfig* with cluster administrator credentials, many users tend to use these generated credentials for much more than their intended use. These credentials should be used only for bootstrapping a cluster. Any production deployment should always configure additional identity mechanisms, and these will be discussed in Chapter 7.

Taints

For production use cases, we recommend that user workloads be isolated from the control plane components. As such, kubeadm taints all control plane nodes with the `node-role.kubernetes.io/master` taint. This instructs the scheduler to ignore all nodes with this taint, when determining where a Pod may be placed.

If your use case is that of a single-node master, you may remove this restriction by removing the taint from the node:

```
kubectl taint nodes <node name> node-role.kubernetes.io/master-
```

Installing Worker Nodes

Worker nodes follow a very similar installation mechanism. Again, we require the container runtime and the kubelet on every node. But, for workers, the only other Kubernetes component that we need is the `kube-proxy` daemon. And, just as with the control plane nodes, kubeadm starts this process by way of another static manifest.

Most significantly, this process performs a TLS bootstrapping sequence. Through a shared token exchange process, kubeadm temporarily authenticates the node against the API server and then attempts to perform a certificate signing request (CSR) against the control plane CA. After the node's credentials have been signed, these serve as the authentication mechanism at runtime.

This sounds complex, but, again, kubeadm makes this process extraordinarily simple:

```
$ kubeadm join --token <token> --discovery-token-ca-cert-hash <hash> \
    <api endpoint>
```

Although not as simple as the control plane case, it is pretty straightforward nonetheless. And, in the case where you use kubeadm manually, the output from the `kubeadm init` command even provides the precise command that needs to be run on a worker node.

Obviously, if we are asking a worker node to join itself to the Kubernetes cluster, we need to tell it where to register itself. That is where the `<api endpoint>` parameter comes in. This includes the IP (or domain name) and port of the API server.

Since this mechanism allows for a node to initiate the join, we want to ensure that this action is secure. For obvious reasons, we do not want just any node to be able to join the cluster, and similarly, we want the worker node to be able to verify the authenticity of the control plane. This is where the `--token` and `--discovery-token-ca-cert-hash` parameters come into play.

The `--token` parameter is a bootstrap token that has been predefined with the control plane. In our simple use case, a bootstrap token has been automatically allocated by way of the `kubeadm init` invocation. Users may also create these bootstrap tokens on the fly:

```
$ kubeadm token create [--ttl <duration>]
```

This mechanism is especially handy when adding new worker nodes to the cluster. In this case, the steps are simply to use `kubeadm token create` to define a new bootstrap token and then use that token in a `kubeadm join` command on the new worker node.

The `--discovery-token-ca-cert-hash` provides the worker node a mechanism to validate the CA of the control plane. By presharing the SHA256 hash of the CA, the worker node may validate that the credentials it received, were, in fact, from the intended control plane.

The whole command may look something like this:

```
$ kubeadm join --token 878b76.ddab3219269370b2 10.1.2.15:6443 \
    --discovery-token-ca-cert-hash \
    sha256:312ce807a9e98d544f5a53b36ae3bb95cdcbe50cf8d1294d22ab5521ddb54d68
```

Add-Ons

After you install the control plane and bring up a few worker nodes, the obvious next step is to get some workloads deployed. Before we can do so, we need to deploy a few add-ons.

Minimally, we need to install a Container Network Interface (CNI) plug-in. This plug-in provides Pod-to-Pod (also known as *east-west*) network connectivity. There are a multitude of options out there, each with their own specific life cycles, so kubeadm stays out of the business of trying to manage them. In the simplest of cases, this is a matter of applying the `DaemonSet` manifest outlined by your CNI provider.

Additional add-ons that you might want in your production clusters would probably include log aggregation, monitoring, and maybe even service mesh capabilities. Again, since these can be complex, kubeadm does not attempt to manage them.

The one special add-on that kubeadm manages is that of cluster DNS. kubeadm currently supports `kube-dns` and `CoreDNS`, with `kube-dns` being the default. As with all parts of kubeadm, you may even choose to forego these standard options and install the cluster DNS provider of your choosing.

Phases

As we alluded to earlier in the chapter, kubeadm serves as the basis for a variety of other Kubernetes installation tools. As you might imagine, if we are trying to make use of kubeadm in this way, we may want some parts of the installation to be managed by kubeadm and others to be handled by the wrapping installer framework. kubeadm supports this use case, as well, with a feature called phases.

With phases, a user may leverage kubeadm to perform discrete actions undertaken in the installation process. For instance, maybe the wrapping tool would like to use kubeadm for its ability to generate PKI assets. Or perhaps that tool wants to leverage kubeadm's preflight checks in order to ensure that a cluster has best practices in place. All of this—and more—is available with kubeadm phases.

High Availability

If you have been paying close attention, you probably noticed that we haven't spoken about a highly available control plane. That is somewhat intentional.

As the purview of kubeadm is primarily from the perspective of a single node at a time, evolving kubeadm into a general-use tool for managing highly available installs would be relatively complicated. Doing so would start to blur the lines of the Unix philosophy of "doing one thing, and doing it well."

That said, kubeadm can be (and is) used to provide the components necessary for a highly available control plane. Although there are a number of precise (and sometimes nuanced) actions that a user needs to take in order to create a highly available control plane, the basic steps are:

1. Create a highly available etcd cluster.
2. Initialize a primary control plane node with `kubeadm init` and a configuration that makes use of the etcd cluster created in step 1.
3. Transfer the PKI assets securely to all of the other control plane nodes.
4. Front the control plane API servers with a load balancer.

5. Join all workers nodes to the cluster by way of the load-balanced endpoints.

 If this is your use case, and you would like to use kubeadm to install a production-grade, highly available cluster, be sure to consult kubeadm high availability documentation. This documentation is maintained with each release of Kubernetes.

Upgrades

As with any deployment, there will come a time when you want to take advantage of all the new features that Kubernetes has to offer. Similarly, if you require a critical security update, you want the ability to enable it with as little disruption as possible. Fortunately, Kubernetes provides for zero-downtime upgrades. Your applications continue to run while the underlying infrastructure is modified.

Although there are countless ways to upgrade a cluster, we focus on the kubeadm use case—a feature that has been available since version 1.8.

There are a lot of moving parts in any Kubernetes cluster, and this can make orchestrating the upgrade complicated. kubeadm simplifies this significantly, as it is able to track well-tested version combinations for the kubelet, etcd, and the container images that serve the Kubernetes control plane.

The order of operations when performing an upgrade is straightforward. First, we plan our upgrade, and then we apply our determined plan.

During the plan phase, kubeadm analyzes the running cluster and determines the possible upgrade paths. In the simplest case, we upgrade to a minor or patch release (e.g., from 1.10.3 to 1.10.4). Slightly more complicated is the upgrade to a whole new minor release that is two (or more) releases forward (e.g., 1.8 to 1.10). In this case, we need to walk the upgrades through each successive minor version until we reach our desired state.

kubeadm performs a number of preflight checks to ensure that the cluster is healthy and then examines the kubeadm-config ConfigMap in the kube-system namespace. This ConfigMap helps kubeadm determine the available upgrade paths and ensures that any custom configuration items are carried forward.

Although much of the heavy lifting happens automatically, you may recall that the kubelet (and kubeadm itself) is not managed by kubeadm. When performing the plan, kubeadm indicates which unmanaged components also need to be upgraded:

```
root@control1:~# kubeadm upgrade plan
[preflight] Running pre-flight checks.
[upgrade] Making sure the cluster is healthy:
[upgrade/config] Making sure the configuration is correct:
```

```
[upgrade/config] Reading configuration from the cluster...
[upgrade/config] FYI: You can look at this config file with
'kubectl -n kube-system get cm kubeadm-config -oyaml'
[upgrade/plan] computing upgrade possibilities
[upgrade] Fetching available versions to upgrade to
[upgrade/versions] Cluster version: v1.9.5
[upgrade/versions] kubeadm version: v1.10.4
[upgrade/versions] Latest stable version: v1.10.4
[upgrade/versions] Latest version in the v1.9 series: v1.9.8

Components that must be upgraded manually after you have upgraded
the control plane with 'kubeadm upgrade apply':
COMPONENT    CURRENT      AVAILABLE
Kubelet      4 x v1.9.3   v1.9.8

Upgrade to the latest version in the v1.9 series:

COMPONENT           CURRENT    AVAILABLE
API Server          v1.9.5     v1.9.8
Controller Manager  v1.9.5     v1.9.8
Scheduler           v1.9.5     v1.9.8
Kube Proxy          v1.9.5     v1.9.8
Kube DNS            1.14.8     1.14.8

You can now apply the upgrade by executing the following command:

        kubeadm upgrade apply v1.9.8

_____

Components that must be upgraded manually after you have upgraded
the control plane with 'kubeadm upgrade apply':
COMPONENT    CURRENT      AVAILABLE
Kubelet      4 x v1.9.3   v1.10.4

Upgrade to the latest stable version:

COMPONENT           CURRENT    AVAILABLE
API Server          v1.9.5     v1.10.4
Controller Manager  v1.9.5     v1.10.4
Scheduler           v1.9.5     v1.10.4
Kube Proxy          v1.9.5     v1.10.4
Kube DNS            1.14.8     1.14.8

You can now apply the upgrade by executing the following command:

        kubeadm upgrade apply v1.10.4

_____
```

You should upgrade system components consistent with the manner in which they were installed (typically with the OS package manager).

After you have determined your planned upgrade approach, begin to execute the upgrades in the order specified by kubeadm. If there are multiple releases in the upgrade path, perform those on each node, as indicated.

```
root@control1:~# kubeadm upgrade apply v1.10.4
```

Again, preflight checks are performed, primarily to ensure that the cluster is still healthy, backups of the various static Pod manifests are made, and the upgrade takes place.

In terms of node order, ensure that you upgrade the control plane nodes first and then perform the upgrades on each worker node. Control plane nodes should be unregistered as upstreams for any front-facing load balancers, upgraded, and then, after the entire control plane has been successfully upgraded, all control plane nodes should be re-registered as upstreams with the load balancer. This may introduce a short-lived period of time when the API is unavailable, but it ensures that all clients have a consistent experience.

If you are performing upgrades for each worker in place, the workers may be upgraded in parallel. Note that this may result in a period of time when there are no kubelets available for scheduling Pods. Alternatively, you may upgrade workers in a rolling fashion. This ensures that there is always a node that may be deployed to.

 If your upgrade also involves simultaneously performing disruptive upgrades on the worker nodes (e.g., upgrading the kernel), it is advisable to use the kubectl cordon and/or kubectl drain semantics to ensure that your user workloads are rescheduled prior to the maintenance.

Summary

In this chapter, we looked at how to easily install Kubernetes across a number of use cases. Although we have only scratched the surface with regard to what kubeadm is capable of, we hope we have demonstrated what a versatile tool it can be.

Since many of the deployment tools available today have kubeadm as an underpinning, knowing how it works should help you understand what higher-order tools are doing on your behalf. And, if you are so inclined, this understanding can help you develop your own in-house deployment tooling.

## CHAPTER 7

Authentication and User Management

Now that we have successfully installed Kubernetes, one of the most fundamental aspects of a successful deployment centers around consistent user management. As with any multitenant, distributed system, user management forms the basis for how Kubernetes ultimately authenticates identities, determines appropriate levels of access, enables self-service capabilities, and maintains auditability.

In this chapter and the next, we explore how to make the best use of the authentication and access control capabilities of Kubernetes. But to get a true understanding of how these constructs work, it is important to first understand the life cycle of an API request.

Every API request that makes its way to the API server needs to successfully navigate a series of challenges, as illustrated in Figure 7-1, before the server will accept (and subsequently act) on the request. Each of these tests falls into one of three groups: authentication, access control, and admission control.

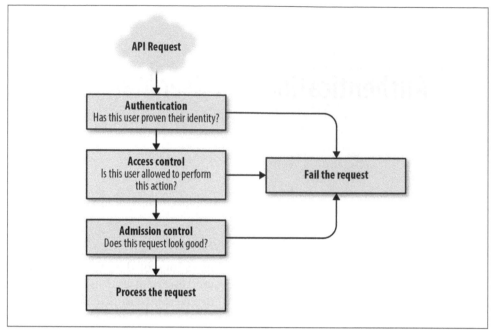

Figure 7-1. Kubernetes API request flow

The number and complexity of these challenges depends on how the Kubernetes API server is configured, but best practices call for production clusters to implement all three in some form or fashion.

The first two phases of servicing an API request (authentication and access control) focus on what we know about a user. In this chapter, we offer an understanding of what a user is from the perspective of the API server and, ultimately, how to leverage user resources to provide secure API access to the cluster.

Users

The term *users* pertains to how you and I (and maybe even your continuous delivery tooling) connect and gain access to the Kubernetes API. In the most common case, users are often connecting to the Kubernetes API from some external place, often by way of the `kubectl` command-line interface. However, since the Kubernetes API forms the basis for all interactions with the cluster, these controls are also in place for all kinds of access—your custom scripts and controllers, the web user interface, and much more. This provides a consistent, secure position from which to start.

You may have noticed that, until now, we have refrained from using a capital "U" when referring to users. Many newcomers to Kubernetes are often surprised to learn that, among the wide array of resources provided by the API, users are, in fact, not a top-level supported resource. They are not manipulated directly by way of the Kubernetes API, but, most commonly, are defined in an external user identity management system.

There is good reason for this—it stands in support of good user management hygiene. If you are like the vast majority of organizations that have deployed Kubernetes, you almost certainly already have some form of user management in place. Whether this comes in the form of a corporate-wide Active Directory cluster or a one-off Lightweight Directory Access Protocol (LDAP) server, how you manage your users should remain consistent across your organization, regardless of the systems consuming it. Kubernetes supports this design tenet by providing the connectivity to leverage these existing systems, thus enabling consistent and effective user management across your infrastructure.

 The absence of such systems does not mean that you won't be able to use Kubernetes. It may just mean that you may need to leverage a different mechanism for authenticating users, as we will discover in the following section.

Authentication

At the time of this writing, Kubernetes supports multiple ways of authenticating against the API. As with any authentication mechanism, this serves as the first gatekeeper for any kind of programatic access. The questions we are evaluating here are, "Who is this user?" and "Do their credentials match our expectations?" At this point in the API flow we are not yet concerned about whether the request *should* be granted based on the user's role or even whether the request conforms to our standards. The question here is simple, and the answer binary: "Is this a genuine user?"

Just as with many well-designed REST-based APIs, there are multiple strategies that Kubernetes can employ for authenticating users. We can think about each of these strategies as belonging to one of three major groups:

- Basic Authentication
- X.509 client certificates
- Bearer tokens

The way that a user ultimately arrives at obtaining credentials depends on the identity provider enabled by the cluster administrator, but the mechanism will adhere to one of these broad groups. And although these mechanisms are vastly different in terms of how they are implemented, we will come to see how each ultimately provides the API server with the data it needs to verify the authenticity and access levels of a user (by way of the UserInfo resource).

Basic Authentication

Basic Authentication is perhaps the most primitive of the authentication plug-ins available to a Kubernetes cluster. Basic Authentication is a mechanism whereby the API client (typically kubectl) sets the HTTP Authorization header to a base64 hash of the combined username and password. Since base64 is merely a hash and provides no level of encryption for the transmitted credentials, it is imperative that Basic Authentication be used in conjunction with HTTPS.

To configure Basic Authentication on the API server, the administrator needs to supply a static file of usernames, passwords, user IDs, and a list of groups that this user should be associated with. The format is as follows:

```
password,username,uid,"group1,group2,group3"
password,username,uid,"group1,group2,group3"
...
```

Note that the format of these lines matches the fields of the UserInfo resource.

This file is supplied to the Kubernetes API server by way of the --basic-auth-file command-line parameter. Since the API server does not currently monitor this file for changes, whenever a user is added, removed, or updated, the API server needs to be restarted in order for these changes to take effect. Because of this constraint, Basic Authentication is not normally recommended for production clusters. This file may certainly be managed by an external entity (e.g., configuration management tooling) in order to get to production-like configurations, but experience shows that this quickly becomes unsustainable.

These shortcomings aside, it should be noted that Basic Authentication can be a excellent tool for a fast and straightforward test of a Kubernetes cluster. In the absence of a more elaborate authentication configuration, Basic Authentication allows an administrator to quickly experiment with features like access control.

X.509 client certificates

An authentication mechanism that is typically enabled by most of Kubernetes installers is X.509 client certificates. The reasons for this may be many, but it is almost certainly due to the fact that they are secure, ubiquitous, and may be generated relatively easily. If there is access to a signing CA, new users can be created in short order.

When installing Kubernetes in a production-quality manner, we want to be sure that not only are user-initiated requests transmitted securely, but also that service-to-service communication is encrypted. X.509 client certificates make perfect sense for this use case. So, if this is already a requirement, why not use it to authenticate users, as well?

This is precisely how many of the installation tools work. For example, kubeadm, the community-supported installer, creates a self-signed root CA certificate and then uses this for signing various certificates for the service components as well as the single administrative certificate that it creates.

A single certificate for all of your users is not the best way to manage users within Kubernetes, but it will do for getting things up and running. When the need to onboard additional users arises, administrators may sign additional client certificates from this signing authority.

 Since kubeadm is intended to be both an easy on-ramp for users to stand up a cluster and a tool for building production-grade clusters, it is highly configurable. For instance, users require the use of their own CA, they may configure kubeadm to sign certificates for both the service and user authentication requirements.

There are a variety of tools that can help an administrator create and manage client certificates. Some of the more popular choices are the OpenSSL client tools and a utility from Cloudflare, named cfssl (*https://github.com/cloudflare/cfssl*). If you are already familiar with these tools, you know that the command-line options can sometimes be a bit cumbersome. We focus on cfssl here, since it has, in our opinion, a workflow that is a bit easier to grasp.

We assume that you already have an existing signing CA. The first step is to create a CSR, which will be used to generate the client certificate. Again, we need to map a user's identity to a UserInfo resource. We can do so with the signing request. Here, our specification of Common Name CN maps to username, and all Organization fields O map to the groups that the user is a member of.

```
cat > joesmith-csr.json <<EOF
{
  "CN": "joesmith",
  "key": {
    "algo": "rsa",
    "size": 2048
  },
  "names": [
    {
      "C": "US",
      "L": "Boston",
      "O": "qa",
      "O": "infrastructure",
      "OU": "Acme Sprockets Company",
      "ST": "MA"
    }
  ]
}
```

In this case, the user "joesmith" is a member of both "qa" and "infrastructure".

We can generate the certificate as follows:

```
cfssl gencert \
  -ca=ca.pem \
  -ca-key=ca-key.pem \
  -config=ca-config.json \
  -profile=kubernetes \
  joesmith-csr.json | cfssljson -bare admin
```

Enabling X.509 client certificate authentication on the API server is as simple as specifying the `--client-ca-file=`, the value of which will point at the certificate file on disk.

Even though `cfssl` simplifies the task of creating client certificates, this means of authentication can still be a bit unwieldy. Just as with basic authentication, there are some drawbacks when a user is onboarded, removed, or when a change is required (e.g., adding a user to a new group). If certificates are chosen as an authentication option, administrators should, minimally, be sure that this process is automated in some fashion and that this automation includes a process for rotating certificates over time.

If the number of expected end users is quite low, or if the majority of users will interact with the cluster by way of some intermediary (e.g., continuous delivery tools), X.509 client certificates may be an adequate solution. If this is not the case, however, you may find some of the token-based options to be a bit more flexible.

OpenID Connect

OIDC is an authentication layer built on top of OAuth 2.0. With this authentication provider, the user independently authenticates with a trusted identity provider. If this user successfully authenticates, the provider then, through a series of web requests, provides the user with one or more tokens.

 Because this exchange of codes and tokens is somewhat complex and is not really pertinent to how Kubernetes authenticates and authorizes the user, we focus on the desired state, where the user has authenticated and both an `id_token` and a `refresh_token` have been granted.

The tokens are provided to the user in the RFC 7519 JSON Web Token (JWT) format. This open standard allows for the representation of user claims between multiple parties. Put more simply, with a trivial amount of human-parsable JSON, we can share information, such as username, user ID, and the groups this user may belong to. These tokens are authenticated with a Hash-based Message Authentication Code (HMAC) and are not encrypted. So, again, be sure that all communication including JWT is encrypted, preferably with TLS.

A typical token payload looks something like this:

```
{
  "iss": "https://auth.example.com",
  "sub": "Ch5hdXRoMHwMTYzOTgzZTdjN2EyNWQxMDViNjESBWF1N2Q2",
  "aud": "dDblg7x07dks1uG60p976jC7TjUZDCDz",
  "exp": 1517266346,
  "iat": 1517179946,
  "at_hash": "OjgZQ0vauibNVcXP52CtoQ",
  "username": "user",
  "email": "user@example.com",
  "email_verified": true,
  "groups": [
    "qa",
    "infrastructure"
  ]
}
```

The fields in this JSON document are called *claims*, and they serve to identify various attributes of the user. Although many of these claims are standardized (e.g., iss, iat, exp), identity providers may also add their own custom claims. Fortunately, the API server allows us to indicate how these claims will map back to our UserInfo resource.

To enable OIDC authentication on the API server, we need to add the --oidc-issuer-url and --oidc-client-id parameters on the command line. These are the URL of the identity provider and the ID of the client configuration, respectively, and both of these values are given by your provider. The two other options that we may want to configure, though this is not mandatory, are --oidc-username-claim (default: sub) and --oidc-group-claim (default: groups). It's great if these defaults match the structure of your tokens. But even if they don't match, each allows you to map claims on the identity provider to their respective UserInfo attributes.

 There is a fantastic tool for examining the structure of JWTs (*https://jwt.io*). This tool from Auth0 not only allows you to paste your token for exploration of its contents but also offers an in-depth reference of open source JWT signing and verification libraries.

This type of authentication is a bit different than the others that we have looked at in that it involves an intermediary. With basic authentication and X.509 client certificates, the Kubernetes API server is able to perform all of the steps required for authentication. As shown in Figure 7-2, with OIDC, the end user authenticates against our mutually trusted identity provider and then use the tokens she has received to subsequently prove her identity to the API server. The flow looks something like the illustration in Figure 7-2.

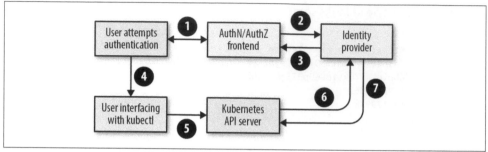

Figure 7-2. Kubernetes OIDC flow

1. The user authenticates and authorizes the Kubernetes API server application.

2. The authentication frontend passes the user's credentials on to the identity provider.

3. If the identity provider is able to authenticate the user, the provider returns an access code. This access code is then returned to the identity provider and exchanged for an identity token and (usually) a refresh token.

4. The user adds these tokens to the *kubeconfig* configuration.

5. Now that the *kubeconfig* file contains OIDC identity information, kubectl attempts to inject the token as a bearer token on each Kubernetes API request. If the token is expired, kubectl will first attempt to get a new identity token by exchanging the expired identity token with the issuer.

6. The Kubernetes API server ensures that this token is legitimate by requesting user information from the identity provider, based on the token credentials.

7. If the token is validated, the identity provider returns user information and the Kubernetes API server allows the original Kubernetes API request to continue its flow.

Webhook

In some scenarios, an administrator already has access to systems that are capable of generating bearer tokens. You might be able to imagine a scenario where an in-house system grants a user a long-lived token that he or she may be able to use to authenticate to any number of systems within the environment. It may not be as elaborate or standards-compliant as OIDC, but as long as we can programmatically challenge the authenticity of that token, Kubernetes is able to verify the identity of a user.

With webhook authentication in place, the API server extracts any bearer token present on an inbound request and subsequently issues a client POST request to the

authentication service. The body of this request will be a JSON serialized `TokenRe
view` resource embedded with the original bearer token.

```
{
  "apiVersion": "authentication.k8s.io/v1beta1",
  "kind": "TokenReview",
  "spec": {
    "token": "some-bearer-token-string"
  }
}
```

After the authenticating service evaluates this token for authenticity, it is then
required to formulate its own response, again, with a `TokenReview` as the body. The
response indicates, with a simple `true` or `false`, whether the bearer token is legitimate. If the request fails authentication, the response is a simple one:

```
{
  "apiVersion": "authentication.k8s.io/v1beta1",
  "kind": "TokenReview",
  "status": {
    "authenticated": false
  }
}
```

If there was an error in authenticating the user for some reason, the
service may also respond with an `error` string field as a sibling to
`authenticated`.

Conversely, if the response is that the authentication was successful, the provider
should respond, minimally, with data about the user with an embedded `UserInfo`
resource object. This object has fields for `username`, `uid`, `groups`, and even one for
`extra` data the service may want to pass along.

```
{
  "apiVersion": "authentication.k8s.io/v1beta1",
  "kind": "TokenReview",
  "status": {
    "authenticated": true,
    "user": {
      "username": "janedoe@example.com",
      "uid": "42",
      "groups": [
        "developers",
        "qa"
      ],
      "extra": {
        "extrafield1": [
          "extravalue1",
```

```
            "extravalue2"
        ]
      }
    }
  }
}
```

Once the API initiates the request and receives a response, the API server grants or denies the Kubernetes API request, in accordance with the guidance provided by the authentication service.

 One thing to keep in mind with nearly all of the token-based authentication mechanisms is that verification of the token often involves an additional request and response. In the case of both OIDC and webhook authentication, for instance, this additional roundtrip to authenticate the token may become a performance bottleneck for the API request if the identity provider does not respond in timely fashion. With any of these plug-ins in play, be sure that you have low-latency and performant providers.

Featured project: dex

What happens when none of these services are appropriate for your use case? You may have noticed that commonly utilized directory services are not included in the list of natively supported authentication plug-ins for Kubernetes. For example, at the time of this writing, there are no connectors for Active Directory, LDAP, or others.

Of course, you *could* always write your own authenticating proxy that would interface with these systems, but that would quickly become yet another piece of infrastructure to develop, manage, and maintain.

Enter dex (*https://github.com/coreos/dex*), a project from CoreOS that may be used as an OIDC broker. dex provides a standards-compliant OIDC frontend to a variety of common backends. There is support for LDAP, Active Directory, SQL, SAML, and even SaaS providers, such as GitHub, GitLab, and LinkedIn. Just imagine your delight when you receive that invite from your Kubernetes administrator:

```
I'd like to add you to my professional Kubernetes cluster network on LinkedIn.
```

It is important to note that the authentication mechanisms configured in a Kubernetes cluster are not mutually exclusive. In fact, we recommend enabling multiple plug-ins simultaneously.

As an administrator, you may, for instance, configure both TLS client certificate and OIDC authentication at the same time. Although it is probably not appropriate to use multiple mechanisms on a daily basis, such a configuration may prove valuable when you need to debug a failing secondary API authentication mechanism. In this scenario, you can leverage a well-known (and hopefully protected) certificate to garner additional data on the failure.

Note that when multiple authentication plug-ins are active at the same time, the first plug-in to successfully authenticate a user will shortcircuit the authentication process.

kubeconfig

With all of the authentication mechanisms we have described, we need to craft a *kubeconfig* file that records the details of how we authenticate. kubectl uses this configuration file to determine where and how to issue requests to the API server. This file is typically located in your home directory under *~/.kube/config* but may also be specified explicitly on the command line with the --kubeconfig parameter or by way of the KUBECONFIG environment variable.

Whether or not you embed your credentials in your *kubeconfig* depends on which authentication mechanism you use and possibly even your security stance. Remember that, if you do embed credentials into this configuration file, they may be used by anyone who has access to this file. Treat this file as if it were a highly sensitive password, because it effectively is.

For someone who may not be familiar with a *kubeconfig* file, it is important to understand its three top-level structures: users, clusters, and contexts. With users we name a user and provide the mechanism by which he or she will authenticate to a cluster. The clusters attribute provides all of the data necessary to connect to a cluster. This, minimally, includes the IP or fully qualified domain name for the API server but may also include items like the CA bundle for a self-signed certificate. And contexts is where we associate users with clusters as a single named entity. The context serves as the means by which kubectl connects and authenticates to an API server.

All of your credentials for all of your clusters may be represented with a single *kubeconfig* configuration. Best of all, this is manipulated by way of a few kubectl commands:

```
$ export KUBECONFIG=mykubeconfig
$ kubectl config set-credentials cluster-admin --username=admin \
    --password=somepassword
```

```
User "cluster-admin" set.
$ kubectl config set-credentials regular-user --username=user \
    --password=someotherpassword
User "regular-user" set.
$ kubectl config set-cluster cluster1 --server=https://10.1.1.3
Cluster "cluster1" set.
$ kubectl config set-cluster cluster2 --server=https://192.168.1.50
Cluster "cluster2" set.
$ kubectl config set-context cluster1-admin --cluster=cluster1 \
    --user=cluster-admin
Context "cluster1-admin" created.
$ kubectl config set-context cluster1-regular --cluster=cluster1 \
    --user=regular-user
Context "cluster1-regular" created.
$ kubectl config set-context cluster2-regular --cluster=cluster2 \
    --user=regular-user
Context "cluster2-regular" created.
$ kubectl config view
apiVersion: v1
clusters:
- cluster:
    server: https://10.1.1.3
  name: cluster1
- cluster:
    server: https://192.168.1.50
  name: cluster2
contexts:
- context:
    cluster: cluster1
    user: cluster-admin
  name: cluster1-admin
- context:
    cluster: cluster1
    user: regular-user
  name: cluster1-regular
- context:
    cluster: cluster2
    user: regular-user
  name: cluster2-regular
current-context: ""
kind: Config
preferences: {}
users:
- name: cluster-admin
  user:
    password: somepassword
    username: admin
- name: regular-user
  user:
    password: someotherpassword
    username: user
```

Here, we have created two user definitions, two cluster definitions, and three contexts. And now, with just one more `kubectl`, we can reset our context with a single additional command.

```
$ kubectl config use-context cluster2-regular
Switched to context "cluster2-regular".
```

This makes it extraordinarily simple to change from one cluster to the next, switch both cluster and user, or even impersonate a different user on the same cluster (something that is quite useful to have in an administrator's toolbox).

Although this was a very simple example utilizing basic authentication, users and clusters may be configured with all kinds of options. And these configurations can become relatively complex. That said, this is a powerful tool made simple with a few command-line operations. Utilize the contexts that make the most sense for your use case.

Service Accounts

So far in this chapter, we have discussed how users authenticate with the API. And, in that time, we have only really focused on authentication as it applies to a user that is external to a cluster. Perhaps this is you, executing a `kubectl` command from your console or even with a click through the web interface.

There is another important use case to consider though, and this pertains to how the processes running inside a Pod access the API. At first, you might ask yourself why a process running in the context of a Pod might require API access.

A Kubernetes cluster is a state machine made up of a collection of controllers. Each of these controllers is responsible for reconciling the state of the user-specified resources. So, in the most fundamental case, we need to provide API access for any custom controllers that we intend to implement. But access to the Kubernetes API from a controller is not the only use case. There are countless reasons why a Pod might require self-awareness or even awareness about the cluster as a whole.

The way that Kubernetes handles these use cases is using the `ServiceAccount` resource:

```
$ kubectl create sa testsa
$ kubectl get sa testsa -oyaml
apiVersion: v1
kind: ServiceAccount
metadata:
  name: testsa
  namespace: default
secrets:
- name: testsa-token-nr6md
```

You can think of ServiceAccounts as namespaced user accounts for all Pod resources.

In the output above, note that when we created the ServiceAccount, a Secret named testsa-token-nr6md was also created automatically. Just as with the end-user authentication we discussed earlier, this is the token that will be included as a bearer token on every API request. These credentials are mounted into the Pod in a well-known location that is accessible by the various Kubernetes clients.

```
$ kubectl run busybox --image=busybox -it -- /bin/sh
If you don't see a command prompt, try pressing enter.
/ # ls -al /var/run/secrets/kubernetes.io/serviceaccount
total 4
drwxrwxrwt    3 root      root        140 Feb 11 20:17 .
drwxr-xr-x    3 root      root       4096 Feb 11 20:17 ..
drwxr-xr-x    2 root      root        100 Feb 11 20:17 \
        ..2982_11_02_20_17_08.558803709
lrwxrwxrwx    1 root      root         31 Feb 11 20:17 ..data ->
..2982_11_02_20_17_08.558803709
lrwxrwxrwx    1 root      root         13 Feb 11 20:17 ca.crt -> ..data/ca.crt
lrwxrwxrwx    1 root      root         16 Feb 11 20:17 namespace -> \
        ..data/namespace
lrwxrwxrwx    1 root      root         12 Feb 11 20:17 token -> ..data/token
```

Even though we are attempting to authenticate a process, we again use JWTs, and the claims within look a lot like what we saw in the end-user token scenarios. Recall that one of the API server's objectives is to map data about this user to a UserInfo resource, and this case is no different:

```
{
  "iss": "kubernetes/serviceaccount",
  "kubernetes.io/serviceaccount/namespace": "default",
  "kubernetes.io/serviceaccount/secret.name": "testsa-token-nr6md",
  "kubernetes.io/serviceaccount/service-account.name": "testsa",
  "kubernetes.io/serviceaccount/service-account.uid":
      "23fe204f-0f66-11e8-85d0-080027da173d",
  "sub": "system:serviceaccount:default:testsa"
}
```

Every Pod that is launched has an associated ServiceAccount.

```
apiVersion: v1
kind: Pod
metadata:
  name: testpod
spec:
  serviceAccountName: testpod-sa
```

If none is specified in the Pod manifest, a default ServiceAccount is used. This default ServiceAccount is available on a namespace-wide basis and is automatically created when a namespace is.

There are many scenarios where it is inappropriate, from a security perspective, to provide a Pod with access to the Kubernetes API. Although it is not possible to prevent a Pod from having an associated `ServiceAccount`, in the next chapter we explore how these use cases may be secured.

Summary

In this chapter, we covered the most commonly deployed end-user authentication mechanisms in Kubernetes. Hopefully one or more of these stood out as something you would be interested in enabling in your environment. If not, there are a handful of others (e.g., static token files, authenticating proxies, and others) that may be implemented. One or more of these will almost certainly fit your needs.

Although you should perform due diligence upfront to onboard your users in a secure and scalable manner, remember that, just as with nearly everything in Kubernetes, these configurations may evolve over time. Use the solution that makes sense for your organization today, knowing that you may adopt additional capabilities seamlessly in the future.

## CHAPTER 8

Authorization

Authentication is only the first challenge for a Kubernetes API request. As we introduced in Chapter 7, there are two additional tests for every request: access control and admission control. Although authentication is a critical component for ensuring that only trusted users can effect change on a cluster, as we explore in this chapter, authentication also becomes the enabler for fine-grained control concerning what those users may do.

Beyond just verifying a user's authenticity and determining levels of access, we also want to be sure that every request conforms to our business needs. Every organization has a number of implemented standards. These policies and procedures help us make sense of the complex infrastructures that are required to bring applications to production environments. In this chapter, we take a look at how Kubernetes stands in support of this with admission controllers.

REST

As we have already covered, the Kubernetes API is a RESTful API. The advantageous properties of a RESTful APIs are many (e.g., scalability and portability), but its simple structure is what enables us to determine levels of access within Kubernetes.

For readers who may not be familiar with REST, the semantics are straightforward: resources are manipulated using verbs. As in traditional languages, if we ask someone to "delete the Pod," we do so with a noun and a verb. REST APIs function in the same way.

To illustrate this concept, let's look precisely at how `kubectl` requests information about a Pod. By simply increasing the log level using the `-v` option, we can get an indepth view of the API calls that `kubectl` is making on our behalf.

```
$ kubectl -v=6 get po testpod
I0202 00:28:31.933993   17487 loader.go:357] Config loaded from file
    /home/ubuntu/.kube/config
I0202 00:28:31.994930   17487 round_trippers.go:436] GET
    https://10.0.0.1:6443/api/v1/namespaces/default/pods/testpod 200 OK
```

In this simple Pod information request, we can see that kubectl has issued a GET request (this is the verb) for the pods/testpod resource. You may also notice that there are other elements of the URL path, such as the version of the API, as well as the namespace that we are querying (default, in this case). These elements add additional context for our request, but suffice it to say that the resource and the verb are the primary actors here.

Those who have encountered REST before will be familiar with the four most basic verbs: Create, Read, Update, and Delete (CRUD). These four actions map directly to the HTTP verbs POST, GET, PUT, and DELETE, respectively, and in turn, make up the vast majority of HTTP requests normally found on the internet.

You may also notice that these verbs look somewhat like the verbs we would use when dealing with Kubernetes resources, and you would be right. We can certainly create, delete, update, and even gather information about a Pod, for instance. Just as with HTTP, these four verbs constitute the most basic elements of how we would interact with Kubernetes resources, but in our case we are not limited to just these four. Within the Kubernetes API, in addition to get, update, delete, and patch, we also have access to the verbs list, watch, proxy, redirect, and deletecollection, when dealing with resources. These are the verbs that kubectl (and any client, for that matter) is using behind the scenes on our behalf.

Resources in Kubernetes are familiar constructs—Pods, Services, and Deployments, among others—that we manipulate by way of those verbs.

Authorization

Just because users are authenticated does not mean that we should give equal access rights to all of them. For example, we may want members of the web development team to have the ability to manipulate the Deployments serving web requests but not the underlying Pods that serve as the units of compute for those Deployments. Or perhaps, even within the web team itself, we might have a group that can create resources and another group that can not. In short, we would like to determine which actions are permissible based upon who the user is and/or which groups she is a member of.

This process is known as *authorization*, and it is the next challenge that Kubernetes tests for every API request. Here, we are asking, "Is this user allowed to perform this action?"

Just as with authentication, authorization is the responsibility of the API server. The API server may be configured to implement various authorization modules using the aptly named `--authorization-mode` argument to the `kube-apiserver` executable.

The API server passes each request to these modules in the order defined by the comma-delimited `--authorization-mode` argument. Each module, in turn, may either weigh in on the decision-making process or choose to abstain. In the case of abstinence, the API request simply moves on to the next module for evaluation. If, however, a module does make a decision, the authorization is terminated and reflects the decision of the authorizing module. If the module denies the request, the user receives an appropriate HTTP 403 (Forbidden) response, and if the request is allowed, the request makes its way to the final step of API flow: admission controller evaluation.

At the time of this writing, there are six authorization modules that may be configured. The simplest and most direct are the `AlwaysAllow` and `AlwaysDeny` modules, and just as the names suggest, these modules allow or deny a request, respectively. Both of these modules are really only suited for test environments.

The `Node` authorization module is responsible for applying the authorization rules that we would like to apply to API requests made by worker nodes. Just like end users, the kubelet processes on each of the nodes perform a variety of API requests. For example, the `Node` status that is presented when you execute `kubectl get nodes` is possible because the kubelet has provided its state to the API server with a `PATCH` request.

```
PATCH https://k8s.example.com:6443/api/v1/nodes/node1.example.com/status 200 OK
```

Obviously, the kubelet should not have access to resources like our web service Pods. This module restricts the capabilities of the kubelet to the subset of requests necessary to maintain a functional worker node.

Role-Based Access Control

The most effective means of user authorization in Kubernetes uses the `RBAC` module. Short for role-based access control, this module allows for the implementation of dynamic access control polices at runtime.

Those who are accustomed to this type of authorization from other frameworks might be groaning by now. The way that some of these frameworks have implemented RBAC is all too often a complicated and convoluted process. When defining levels of access is tedious, it can be tempting to provide coarse-grained access controls, if any at all. Worse, when the configuration of these controls is static or inflexible, you can almost guarantee that they will not be implemented effectively.

Fortunately, Kubernetes makes the definition and implementation of RBAC policies extraordinarily simple. Put succinctly, Kubernetes maps the attributes of the User Info object to the resources and verbs that the user should have access to.

Role and ClusterRole

With the RBAC module, authorization to perform an action on a resource is defined with the Role or ClusterRole resource types. (We will dive into the difference between these resources shortly.) To start, let's first focus only on the Role resource. An implementation of the previous example (where a user has read-write access to Deployments but only read access to Pods) might look something like this:

```
kind: Role
apiVersion: rbac.authorization.k8s.io/v1
metadata:
  name: web-rw-deployment
  namespace: some-web-app-ns
rules:
- apiGroups: [""]
  resources: ["pods"]
  verbs: ["get", "list", "watch"]
- apiGroups: ["extensions", "apps"]
  resources: ["deployments"]
  verbs: ["get", "list", "watch", "create", "update", "patch", "delete"]
```

In this Role configuration, we have created a policy that allows for read-type actions to be applied to Pods and for full read-write access rights for Deployments. This Role would enforce that all changes that happen to the child Pods of a Deployment happen at the Deployment level (e.g., rolling updates or scaling).

The apiGroups field of each rule simply indicates to the API server the namespace of the API that it should act on. (This reflects the API namespace defined in the apiVersion field of your resource definition.)

In the next two fields, resources and verbs, we encounter those REST constructs we discussed earlier. And, in the case of RBAC, we explicitly allow these types of API requests for a user with this web-rw-deployment role. Since rules is an array, we may add as many combinations of permissions as are appropriate. All of these permissions are additive. With RBAC, we can only *grant* actions, and this module otherwise denies by default.

Role and ClusterRole are identical in functionality and differ only in their scope. In the example just shown, you may notice that this policy is bound to the resources in the some-web-app-ns namespace. That means that this policy is only applied to resources in that namespace.

If we want to grant a permission that has cross-namespace capabilities, we use the ClusterRole resource. This resource, in the same manner, grants fine-grained control but on a cluster-wide basis.

You might be wondering why someone would ever want to implement policies like this. ClusterRoles are typically employed for two primary use cases—to easily grant cluster administrators a wide degree of freedom or to grant very specific permissions to a Kubernetes controller.

The first case is simple. We often want administrators to have broad access so that they can easily debug problems. Of course, we could have a Role policy for every namespace that we eventually create, but it may be more expedient to just grant this access with a ClusterRole. Since these permissions are far reaching, we use this construct with caution.

Most Kubernetes controllers are interested in watching resources across namespaces and then reconciling cluster states appropriately. We can use ClusterRole policies to ensure that controllers only have access to the resources they care about.

 All Kubernetes controllers (e.g., Deployments or StatefulSets) have the same basic structure. They are a state machine that watches the Kubernetes API for changes (additions, modification, and deletions) and seeks to reconcile from the current state to the user-specified desired state.

Imagine a scenario where we wanted to create DNS records based upon a user-specified annotation on a Service or Ingress resource. Our controller would need to watch these resources and take action upon some sort of change. It would be insecure to give this controller access to other resources and inappropriate verbs (e.g., DELETE on Pods). We can use a ClusterRole policy to provide the correct level of access as follows:

```
apiVersion: rbac.authorization.k8s.io/v1
kind: ClusterRole
metadata:
  name: external-dns
rules:
- apiGroups: [""]
  resources: ["services"]
  verbs: ["get", "watch", "list"]
- apiGroups: ["extensions"]
  resources: ["ingresses"]
  verbs: ["get", "watch", "list"]
```

And this is exactly how the external-dns Kubernetes incubator project (*http://bit.ly/2Qp5GlP*) works.

With this `ClusterRole` policy in place, an external-dns controller can watch for additions, modifications, or even deletions of `Service` and `Ingress` resources and act on them accordingly. And, most importantly, these controllers do *not* have access to any other aspects of the API.

 Be sure to understand all implications when granting users access rights with RBAC. Always seek to give *only* the rights that are necessary, since this significantly reduces your security exposure. Also understand that some rights grant implicit—and perhaps unintentional—rights to other resources. In particular, you should know that granting `create` rights to a Pod effectively grants read access to more sensitive and related resources, like Secrets. Because Secrets may be mounted or exposed via environment variables to a Pod, the Pod `create` rights allows a Pod owner to read those Secrets unencrypted.

RoleBinding and ClusterRoleBinding

You'll notice that neither `Role` nor `ClusterRole` specify which users or groups to target with their rules. Policies alone are useless unless they are applied to a user or a group. To associate these policies with users, groups, or `ServiceAccounts`, we can use the `RoleBinding` and `ClusterRoleBinding` resources. The only difference here is whether we are trying to bind a `Role` or `ClusterRole`. Again, `RoleBindings` are namespaced.

`RoleBinding` and `ClusterRoleBinding` associate a policy with a subject:

```
kind: RoleBinding
apiVersion: rbac.authorization.k8s.io/v1
metadata:
  name: web-rw-deployment
  namespace: some-web-app-ns
subjects:
- kind: User
  name: "joesmith@example.com"
  apiGroup: rbac.authorization.k8s.io
- kind: Group
  name: "webdevs"
  apiGroup: rbac.authorization.k8s.io
roleRef:
  kind: Role
  name: web-rw-deployment
  apiGroup: rbac.authorization.k8s.io
```

In this example, we have associated the `web-rw-deployment` `Role` in the `some-web-app-ns` namespace to *joesmith@example.com*, as well as to a group with the name web devs.

As you may recall from Chapter 7, the objective of every type of authentication mechanism is two-fold—first, to ensure that the user's credentials match our expectations, and second, to obtain information about an authenticated user. This information is conveyed with the aptly named UserInfo resource. The string values that we specify here are reflective of the user information obtained during authentication.

When it comes to authorization, there are three subject types to which we may apply policy: Users, Groups, and ServiceAccounts. In the case of Users and Groups, these are defined by the UserInfo username and groups fields, respectively.

 The values of these fields are strings, in the case of username, and a list of strings for groups, and the comparison used for inclusion is a simple string match. These string values are up to you, and they can be any unique string values that your authorization system provides to identify a user or group.

ServiceAccounts are specified explicitly with the appropriately named ServiceAccount subject type.

```
...
subjects:
- kind: ServiceAccount
  name: testsa
  namespace: some-web-app-ns
```

Remember that ServiceAccounts supply the Kubernetes API credentials for all running Pod processes. Every Pod has an associated ServiceAccount, regardless of whether we specify which serviceAccountName to use in the Pod manifest. Left unattended, this could pose a significant security concern.

This concern can be largely mitigated with RBAC policies. Since RBAC policies are *default deny*, we recommended that any Pod that requires API capabilities have its own (or possibly shared) ServiceAccount with an associated fine-grained RBAC policy. Only grant this ServiceAccount the actions and resources that it requires to function properly.

Recall the ClusterRole external-dns example. Because the controller state machine issues requests to the Kubernetes API from a Pod context, we can use a ClusterRole Binding with a ServiceAccount subject to enable this functionality:

```
apiVersion: rbac.authorization.k8s.io/v1beta1
kind: ClusterRoleBinding
metadata:
  name: external-dns-binding
roleRef:
  apiGroup: rbac.authorization.k8s.io
  kind: ClusterRole
```

```
    name: external-dns
subjects:
- kind: ServiceAccount
  name: external-dns
  namespace: default
```

Testing Authorization

As the number of users, groups, and workloads on a Kubernetes cluster increases, so
too does the complexity. Although RBAC is a simple mechanism by which to apply
authorization policies to a collection of subjects, implementing and debugging access
rights can sometimes be tough. Fortunately, kubectl provides a handy resource for
verifying our policies without needing to effect any real change on the cluster.

To test access, simply use kubectl to set the context of the user you want to verify (or
a user who is part of a group you need to check).

```
$ kubectl use-context admin
$ kubectl auth can-i get pod
yes
```

Here, we can see that the admin user has GET access to the Pod resource in the
default namespace.

After creating a much more restricted policy, where the user is prevented from creating any Namespace resources (which are scoped at the cluster), we use can-i to con-
firm this policy:

```
$ kubectl use-context basic-user
$ kubectl create namespace mynamespace
Error from server (Forbidden): namespaces is forbidden: User "basic-user"
cannot create namespaces at the cluster scope
$ kubectl auth can-i create namespace
no
```

Note that the user received the appropriate Forbidden when she first attempted to
create the Namespace mynamespace.

> In this chapter, we do not cover the attribute-based access control
> (ABAC) module. This module is semantically very similar to the
> RBAC module, with the exception that these policies are statically
> defined with a configuration file on each of the Kubernetes API
> servers. Just like some of the other file-based configuration items
> we have discussed, this policy is not dynamic. An administrator
> needs to restart the kube-apiserver process each time he wants to
> modify this policy. This aspect makes it impractical for the more
> robust and production-ready RBAC module.

Summary

In this chapter, we covered the RESTful nature of the Kubernetes API and how its structure lends itself well to policy enforcement. We have also explored how authorization directly relates to what we have already covered about authentication.

Authorization is one of the critical components necessary for the deployment of a secure, multitenant distributed system. With RBAC, Kubernetes affords us the capability to enforce both very coarse-grained, sweeping policies and those that are extremely specific to a user or group. And, because Kubernetes makes the definition and maintenance of these policies so trivial to implement, there is really no reason why even the most basic of deployments cannot make use of them. This is a perfect first step toward happy users, administrators, and auditors alike.

## CHAPTER 9

Admission Control

As we mentioned in the previous two chapters, *admission control* is the third phase of API request onboarding. By the time we have reached this phase of an API request life cycle, we have already determined that the request has come from a real, authenticated user and that the user is authorized to perform this request. What we care about now is whether the request meets the criteria for what we consider to be a valid request, and, if not, what action to take. Should we reject the request entirely, or should we alter it to meet our business standards? For those who are familiar with the concept of API middleware, admission controllers are very similar in function.

Although authentication and admission control are both critical to a successful deployment, admission control is where, you, as an administrator, can really start to wrangle your users' workloads. Here, you are able to limit resources, enforce policies, and enable advanced features. This helps to drive utilization, add some sanity to diverse workloads, and seamlessly integrate new technology.

Fortunately, just as with the other two phases, Kubernetes provides a wide array of admission capabilities right out of the box. Although authentication and authorization don't change much between releases, admission control is quite the opposite. There is a seemingly never-ending list of capabilities that users are looking for when it comes to how they administer their clusters. And, because admission control is where most of that magic happens, it is no surprise that this componentry is continually evolving.

We could write books on the native admission control capabilities of Kubernetes. However, because that is not really practical, here we focus on some of the more popular controllers, as well as demonstrate how you can implement your own.

Configuration

Enabling admission control is extremely simple. Since this is an API function, we add the `--enable-admission-plugins` flag to the `kube-apiserver` runtime parameters. This, like other configuration items, is a comma-delimited list of the admission controllers that we want to enable.

 Prior to Kubernetes 1.10, the order in which admission controllers were specified mattered. With the introduction of the `--enable-admission-plugins` command-line parameter, this is no longer the case. For versions 1.9 and earlier, you should use the order-dependent `--admission-control` parameter.

Common Controllers

Much of the functionality that users take for granted in Kubernetes actually happens by way of admission controllers. For example, the `ServiceAccount` admission controller automatically allocates Pods to a `ServiceAccount`. Similarly, if you have tried to add new resources to a `Namespace` that is currently in a terminating state, your request was likely rejected by the `NamespaceLifecycle` controller.

The admission controllers available out of the box from Kubernetes have two primary goals: ensuring that sane defaults are utilized in the absence of user-specified values, and ensuring that users do not have more capabilities than they need. Many of the actions that a user is authorized to perform are controlled with RBAC, but admission controllers allow administrators to define additional fine-grained policies that extend beyond the simplistic resource, action, and subject policies offered by authorization.

PodSecurityPolicies

One of the most widely utilized admission controllers is the `PodSecurityPolicies` controller. With this controller, administrators can specify the constraints of the processes under Kubernetes' control. With `PodSecurityPolicies`, administrators may enforce that Pods are not able to run in a privileged context, that they cannot bind to the `hostNetwork`, must run as a particular user, and that they are constrained by a variety of other security-focused attributes.

When `PodSecurityPolicies` are enabled, users are unable to onboard new Pods unless there are authorized policies in place. Policies may be as permissive or restrictive as required by your organization's security posture. In production multiuser environments, administrators should use most of the policies offered by `PodSecurityPolicies`, since these significantly improve overall cluster security.

Let's consider a simple yet typical case, where we would like to ensure that Pods are not able to run in a privileged context. Defining the policy happens, as usual, by way of the Kubernetes API:

```
apiVersion: policy/v1beta1
kind: PodSecurityPolicy
metadata:
  name: non-privileged
spec:
  privileged: false
```

If you were to create this policy, apply it to the API server, and then attempt to create a conformant Pod, the request would be rejected, since your user and/or the Service Account would not have permission to use the policy. To rectify this situation, simply create an RBAC Role that allows either of those subject types to use this PodSecurity Policy:

```
kind: Role
apiVersion: rbac.authorization.k8s.io/v1
metadata:
  name: non-privileged-user
  namespace: user-namespace
rules:
- apiGroups: ['policy']
  resources: ['podsecuritypolicies']
  verbs:    ['use']
  resources:
  - non-privileged
```

and its RoleBinding:

```
kind: RoleBinding
apiVersion: rbac.authorization.k8s.io/v1
metadata:
  name: non-privileged-user
  namespace: user-namespace
roleRef:
  kind: Role
  name: non-privileged-user
  apiGroup: rbac.authorization.k8s.io
subjects:
- kind: ServiceAccount
  name: some-service-account
  namespace: user-namespace
```

After a user is authorized to use a PodSecurityPolicy, the Pod may be declared as long as it conforms to the policies defined.

Since PodSecurityPolicys are implemented as an admission controller (which enforces policy during the API request flow) Pods that have been scheduled prior to PodSecurityPolicy being enabled may no longer conform. Keep this in mind, since restarts of those Pods may render them unable to be scheduled. Ideally, the PodSecurityPolicy admission controller is enabled at installation time.

ResourceQuota

Generally speaking, it is good practice to enforce *quotas* on your cluster. Quotas ensure that no one user is able to utilize more than she has been allocated and is a critical component in driving overall cluster utilization. If you intend to enforce user quotas, you should also enable the ResourceQuota controller.

This controller ensures that any newly declared Pods are first evaluated against the current quota utilization for the given namespace. By performing this check during workload onboarding, we give immediate notice to a user that his Pod will or will not fit within the quota. Note, too, that when a quota is defined for a namespace, all Pod definitions (even if originating from another resource, such as Deployments or ReplicaSets) are required to specify resource requests and limits.

Quotas may be implemented for an ever-expanding list of resources, but some of the most common include CPU, memory, and volumes. It is also possible to place quotas on the number of distinct Kubernetes resources (e.g., Pods, Deployments, Jobs, and more) within a Namespace.

Configuring quotas is straightforward:

```
$ cat quota.yml
apiVersion: v1
kind: ResourceQuota
metadata:
  name: memoryquota
  namespace: memoryexample
spec:
  hard:
    requests.memory: 256Mi
    limits.memory: 512Mi
```

Now, if we try to exceed the limit, even with a single Pod, our declaration is immediately rejected by the ResourceQuota admission controller:

```
$ cat pod.yml
apiVersion: v1
kind: Pod
metadata:
  name: nginx
  namespace: memoryexample
```

```
    labels:
        app: nginx
spec:
  containers:
  - name: nginx
    image: nginx
    ports:
    - containerPort: 80
    resources:
      limits:
        memory: 1Gi
      requests:
        memory: 512Mi
$ kubectl apply -f pod.yml
Error from server (Forbidden): error when creating "pod.yml": pods "nginx" is
forbidden: exceeded quota: memoryquota, requested:
limits.memory=1Gi,requests.memory=512Mi, used: limits.memory=0,requests.memory=0,
limited: limits.memory=512Mi,requests.memory=256Mi
```

Although somewhat less obvious, the same holds true for Pods created by way of higher-order resources, such as Deployments:

```
$ cat deployment.yml
apiVersion: apps/v1
kind: Deployment
metadata:
  name: nginx-deployment
  namespace: memoryexample
  labels:
    app: nginx
spec:
  replicas: 3
  selector:
    matchLabels:
      app: nginx
  template:
    metadata:
      labels:
        app: nginx
    spec:
      containers:
      - name: nginx
        image: nginx
        ports:
        - containerPort: 80
        resources:
          limits:
            memory: 256Mi
          requests:
            memory: 128Mi
$ kubectl apply -f deployment.yml
deployment.apps "nginx-deployment" configured
$ kubectl get po -n memoryexample
```

```
NAME                                READY   STATUS    RESTARTS   AGE
nginx-deployment-55dd98c6c8-9xmjn   1/1     Running   0          25s
nginx-deployment-55dd98c6c8-hc2pf   1/1     Running   0          24s
```

Even though we have specified three replicas, we could only satisfy two based upon the quota. If we describe the resulting ReplicaSet, we see the failure:

```
Warning  FailedCreate      3s (x4 over 3s)  replicaset-controller
(combined from similar events): Error creating: pods
"nginx-deployment-55dd98c6c8-tkrtz" is forbidden: exceeded quota:
memoryquota, requested: limits.memory=256Mi,requests.memory=128Mi,
used: limits.memory=512Mi,requests.memory=256Mi, limited:
limits.memory=512Mi,requests.memory=256Mi
```

Again, this error is originating from the ResourceQuota admission controller, but this time, the error is somewhat hidden, since it is being returned to the Deployment's ReplicaSet (which is the creator of the Pods).

By now, it is probably becoming clear that quotas can help you effectively manage your resources.

LimitRange

Complementary to ResourceQuota, the LimitRange admission controller is necessary if you have defined any LimitRange policies against a Namespace. A LimitRange, put simply, allows you to place default resource limits for Pods that are declared as a member of a particular Namespace.

```
apiVersion: v1
kind: LimitRange
metadata:
  name: default-mem
spec:
  limits:
  - default:
      memory: 1024Mi
    defaultRequest:
      memory: 512Mi
    type: Container
```

This capability is important in scenarios where quotas have been defined. When quotas are enabled, a user who has not defined resource limits on her Pod has her request rejected. With the LimitRange admission controller, a Pod with no resource limits defined is, instead, given defaults (as defined by the administrator) and the Pod is accepted.

Dynamic Admission Controllers

So far, we have focused on the admission controllers that are available from Kubernetes itself. There may, however, be times when the native functionality just doesn't cut it. In scenarios like this, we need to develop additional functionality that helps us meet our business objectives. Fortunately, Kubernetes supports a wide array of extensibility points, and this is also true for admission controllers.

Dynamic admission control is the mechanism by which we inject custom business logic into the admission control pipeline. There are two types of dynamic admission control: validating and mutating.

With *validating admission control*, our business logic simply accepts or rejects a user's request, based upon our requirements. In the event of failure, an appropriate HTTP status code and reason for failure is returned to the user. We are placing the onus on the end user to declare conformant resource specifications and, hopefully, doing so in a way that does not cause consternation.

In the *mutating admission controller* case, we are again evaluating requests against the API server, but in this case we are selectively altering the declaration to meet our objectives. In simplistic cases, this may be something as straightforward as applying a series of well-known labels to the resource. In more elaborate cases, we may go so far as to transparently inject a sidecar container. While in this case, we are taking on much of the burden for the end user, it can sometimes become a bit confusing for the user when he discovers that some additional magic is happening behind the scenes. That said, this capability, if well-documented, can be critical for implementing advanced architectures.

In both cases, this functionality is implemented using user-defined webhooks. These downstream webhooks are called by the API server when it sees that a qualifying request has been made. (As we will see in the following examples, users are able to qualify requests in a fashion similar to the way in which RBAC policies are defined.) The API server POSTs an AdmissionReview object to these webhooks. The body of this request includes the original request, the status of the object, and metadata about the requesting user.

In turn, the webhook provides a simple AdmissionResponse object. This object includes fields for whether this request is allowed, a reason and code for failure, and even a field for what a mutating patch would look like.

In order to utilize Dynamic Admission Controllers, you must first configure the API server with a change to the --enable-admission-plugins parameter:

```
--enable-admission-plugins=...,MutatingAdmissionWebhook,\
    ValidatingAdmissionWebhook
```

Note that Dynamic Admission Control, although extraordinarily powerful, is still somewhat early in its maturity cycle. These features were alpha as of 1.8 and beta in 1.9. As with all new functionality, be sure to consult the Kubernetes documentation for additional recommendations regarding these extension points.

Validating Admission Controllers

Let's take a look at how we can implement our own validating admission controller and reuse an earlier example. Our controller will inspect all Pod CREATE requests to ensure that each Pod has an environment label and that the label has a value of dev or prod.

To demonstrate that you can write Dynamic Admission Controllers in your language of choice, we use a Python Flask application for this example:

```
import json
import os

from flask import jsonify, Flask, request

app = Flask(__name__)

@app.route('/', methods=['POST'])
def validation():
    review = request.get_json()
    app.logger.info('Validating AdmissionReview request: %s',
                    json.dumps(review, indent=4))

    labels = review['request']['object']['metadata']['labels']
    response = {}
    msg = None
    if 'environment' not in list(labels):
        msg = "Every Pod requires an 'environment' label."
        response['allowed'] = False
    elif labels['environment'] not in ('dev', 'prod',):
        msg = "'environment' label must be one of 'dev' or 'prod'"
        response['allowed'] = False
    else:
        response['allowed'] = True

    status = {
        'metadata': {},
        'message': msg
    }
    response['status'] = status

    review['response'] = response
    return jsonify(review), 200
```

```
    context = (
        os.environ.get('WEBHOOK_CERT', '/tls/webhook.crt'),
        os.environ.get('WEBHOOK_KEY', '/tls/webhook.key'),
    )
    app.run(host='0.0.0.0', port='443', debug=True, ssl_context=context)
```

We containerize this application and make it available internally with a `ClusterIP` Service:

```
---
apiVersion: v1
kind: Pod
metadata:
  name: label-validation
  namespace: infrastructure
  labels:
    controller: label-validator
spec:
  containers:
  - name: label-validator
    image: label-validator:latest
    volumeMounts:
    - mountPath: /tls
      name: tls
  volumes:
  - name: tls
    secret:
      secretName: admission-tls
---
kind: Service
apiVersion: v1
metadata:
  name: label-validation
  namespace: infrastructure
spec:
  selector:
    controller: label-validator
  ports:
  - protocol: TCP
    port: 443
```

In this case, the webhook is hosted on-cluster. For simplicity's sake we have used a standalone Pod, but there is no reason why this couldn't be deployed with something a bit more robust, like a `Deployment`. And, just as with any web service, we secure it with TLS.

After this `Service` becomes available, we need to direct the API server to call our webhook. We indicate which resources and operations we care about, and the API server only calls this webhook when a request that meets this qualification is observed.

```
apiVersion: admissionregistration.k8s.io/v1beta1
kind: ValidatingWebhookConfiguration
metadata:
  name: label-validation
webhooks:
- name: admission.example.com
  rules:
  - apiGroups:
    - ""
    apiVersions:
    - v1
    operations:
    - CREATE
    resources:
    - pods
  clientConfig:
    service:
      namespace: infrastructure
      name: label-validation
    caBundle: <base64 encoded bundle>
```

With a `ValidatingWebhookConfiguration` in place, we can now verify that our policy is working as expected. Attempting to apply a Pod without an `environment` label yields:

```
# kubectl apply -f pod.yaml
Error from server: error when creating "pod.yaml": admission webhook
"admission.example.com" denied the request: Every Pod requires an 'environment'
label.
```

Similarly, with an `environment=staging` label:

```
# kubectl apply -f pod.yaml
Error from server: error when creating "pod.yaml": admission webhook
"admission.example.com" denied the request: 'environment' label must be one of
'dev' or 'prod'
```

It is only when we add an `environment` label according to the specification that we are able to successfully create a new Pod.

> Notice that our application is being served over TLS. As API requests may contain sensitive information, all traffic should be encrypted.

Mutating Admission Controllers

If we modify our example, we can easily develop a mutating webhook. Again, with a mutating webhook we are attempting to alter the resource definition transparently for the user.

In this example, we inject a proxy sidecar container. Although this sidecar is simply a helper `nginx` process, we could modify any aspect of the resource.

 Exercise care when modifying resources at runtime, since there may be existing logic that depends on well-defined and/or previously defined values. A general rule of thumb is to only set previously unset fields. Always avoid altering any namespaced values (e.g., resource annotations).

Our new webhook looks like this:

```
import base64
import json
import os

from flask import jsonify, Flask, request

app = Flask(__name__)

@app.route("/", methods=["POST"])
def mutation():
    review = request.get_json()
    app.logger.info("Mutating AdmissionReview request: %s",
                    json.dumps(review, indent=4))

    response = {}
    patch = [{
        'op': 'add',
        'path': '/spec/containers/0',
        'value': {
            'image': 'nginx',
            'name': 'proxy-sidecar',
        }
    }]
    response['allowed'] = True
    response['patch'] = base64.b64encode(json.dumps(patch))
    response['patchType'] = 'application/json-patch+json'

    review['response'] = response
    return jsonify(review), 200

context = (
    os.environ.get("WEBHOOK_CERT", "/tls/webhook.crt"),
    os.environ.get("WEBHOOK_KEY", "/tls/webhook.key"),
)
app.run(host='0.0.0.0', port='443', debug=True, ssl_context=context)
```

Here, we use the JSON Patch syntax to add the `proxy-sidecar` to the Pod.

Just as with the validating webhook, we containerize the application and then dynamically configure the API server to forward requests to the webhook. The only difference is that we will use a `MutatingWebhookConfiguration` and, naturally, point to the internal ClusterIP Service:

```
apiVersion: admissionregistration.k8s.io/v1beta1
kind: MutatingWebhookConfiguration
metadata:
  name: pod-mutation
webhooks:
- name: admission.example.com
  rules:
  - apiGroups:
    - ""
    apiVersions:
    - v1
    operations:
    - CREATE
    resources:
    - pods
  clientConfig:
    service:
      namespace: infrastructure
      name: pod-mutator
    caBundle: <base64 encoded bundle>
```

Now, when we apply a very simple, single-container Pod, we get something a bit more:

```
# cat pod.yaml
---
apiVersion: v1
kind: Pod
metadata:
  name: testpod
  labels:
    app: testpod
    environment: prod
#staging
spec:
  containers:
  - name: busybox
    image: busybox
    command: ['/bin/sleep', '3600']
```

Even though our Pod declared only the `busybox` container, we now have two containers at runtime:

```
# kubectl get pod testpod
NAME       READY    STATUS     RESTARTS    AGE
testpod    2/2      Running    0           1m
```

And a deeper inspection reveals that our sidecar was injected properly:

```
...
spec:
  containers:
  - image: nginx
    imagePullPolicy: Always
    name: proxy-sidecar
    resources: {}
    terminationMessagePath: /dev/termination-log
    terminationMessagePolicy: File
  - command:
    - /bin/sleep
    - "3600"
    image: busybox
...
```

With mutating webhooks, we have an extremely powerful tool for standardizing our user's declarations. Use this power with caution.

Summary

Admission control is yet another tool for sanitizing your cluster's state. Since this functionality is ever-evolving, be sure to check for new capabilities with every Kubernetes release and to implement those controllers that will help secure your environment and drive utilization. And, where appropriate, don't be afraid to roll up your sleeves, implementing the logic that makes the most sense for your particular use cases.

## CHAPTER 10

Networking

Just as with any distributed system, Kubernetes relies on the network in order to provide connectivity between services, as well as for connecting external users to exposed workloads.

Managing networking in traditional application architectures has always proven quite difficult. In many organizations, there was a segregation of duties—developers would create their applications, and operators would be responsible for running them. Many times, as the application evolved, the needs from the networking infrastructure would drift. In the best of scenarios, the application simply would not operate, and an operator would take corrective action. However, in the worst of scenarios, significant gaps in areas like network security would arise.

Kubernetes allows developers to define network resources and policies that can live alongside their application deployment manifests. These resources and policies may be well scoped by cluster administrators and can leverage any number of best-of-breed technology implementations using common abstraction layers. By removing developers from the nuts and bolts of how the network works, and by colocating the demands of the infrastructure with those of the application, we can have better assurances that our applications can be delivered in a consistent and secure manner.

Container Network Interface

Before we talk about how to connect users with containerized workloads, we need to understand how Pods communicate with other Pods. These Pods may be colocated on the same node, across nodes in the same subnet, and even on nodes in different subnets that are, perhaps, even located in different datacenters. As shown in Figure 10-1, regardless of what the network plumbing looks like, we aim to connect Pods in a seamless, routable manner.

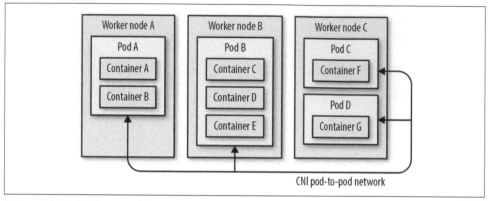

Figure 10-1. CNI networking

Kubernetes interfaces with the network using the CNI specification. The objective of this open specification is to standardize how container orchestration platforms connect containers with the underlying network and to do so in a pluggable way. There are dozens of solutions, each with their own architectures and capabilities. Most are open source solutions, but there are also proprietary solutions from a number of different vendors within the cloud-native ecosystem. Regardless of the environment in which you are deploying your cluster, there will certainly be a plug-in to meet your needs.

Although there are multiple aspects to networking within Kubernetes, the role of CNI is simply to facilitate Pod-to-Pod connectivity. The manner in which this happens is relatively simple. The container runtime (e.g., Docker) calls the CNI plug-in executable (e.g., Calico) to add or remove an interface to or from the container's networking `Namespace`. These are termed *sandbox* interfaces.

As you recall, every Pod is allocated an IP address, and the CNI plug-in is responsible for its allocation and assignment to a Pod.

> You may be asking yourself, "If a Pod can have multiple containers, how does the CNI know which one to connect?" If you have ever interrogated Docker to list the containers running on a given Kubernetes node, you may have noticed a number of `pause` containers associated with each of your Pods. These `pause` containers do nothing meaningful computationally. They merely serve as placeholders for each Pod's container network. As such, they are the first container to be launched and the last to die in the life cycle of an individual Pod.

After the plug-in has executed the desired task on behalf of the container runtime, it returns the status of the execution, just like any other Linux process: `0` for success and any other return code to indicate a failure. As part of a successful operation, the CNI plug-in also returns the details of the IPs, routes, and DNS entries that were manipulated by the plug-in in the process.

In addition to connecting a container to a network, CNI has capabilities for IP Address Management (IPAM). IPAM ensures that CNI always has a clear picture of which addresses are in use, as well as those that are available for configuration of new interfaces.

Choosing a Plug-in

When choosing a CNI plug-in for use in your environment, there are two primary considerations to keep in mind:

What is the topology of your network?
> The topology of your network dictates a large part of what you are ultimately able to deploy within your environment. For instance, if you are deploying to multiple availability zones within a public cloud, you likely need to implement a plug-in that has support for some form of encapsulation (also known as an *overlay network*).

Which features are imperative for your organization?
> You need to consider which features are important for your deployment. If there are hard requirements for mutual TLS between Pods, you may want to use a plug-in that provides this capability. By the same token, not every plug-in provides support for `NetworkPolicy`. Be sure to evaluate the features that are offered by the plug-in before you deploy your cluster.

> The CNI is not the only mechanism for enforcing mutual TLS between Pods. With a sidecar pattern called service mesh, cluster administrators can require that workloads only communicate by a TLS-enabled local proxy. Service mesh not only provides end-to-end encryption but may also enable higher-level features, such as circuit breaking, blue/green deployments, and distributed tracing. It may also be enabled transparently for the end user.

kube-proxy

Even with Pod-to-Pod networking in place, Kubernetes would still be relatively primitive in terms of connectivity if it did not provide some additional abstractions over direct IP-to-IP connectivity. How would we handle the case where a Deployment has multiple replicas and, therefore, multiple serving IPs? Do we just pick one of the IPs and hope it doesn't get removed at some point in the future? Wouldn't it be nice to reference these replicas by a virtual IP? And, taking things one step further, wouldn't it be nice to have a DNS record?

All of this is possible with the Kubernetes `Service` resource that we covered in Chapter 2. With the `Service` resource, we assign a virtual IP for network services exposed by a collection of Pods. The backing Pods are discovered and connected using a Pod selector.

 Many newcomers to Kubernetes typically think of the relationship between a collection of Pods (i.e., a Deployment) and a `Service` as being one-to-one. Because Services are connected to Pods by way of label selectors, any Pod with the appropriate label is considered a `Service` endpoint. This functionality allows you to mix and match backing Pods and can even enable advanced deployments, such as blue/green and canary rollouts.

Behind the scenes, the Kubernetes component that is making all of this possible is the `kube-proxy` process. `kube-proxy` typically runs as a privileged container process, and it is responsible for managing the connectivity for these virtual Service IP addresses.

The name *proxy* is a misnomer of historical origin: `kube-proxy` was originally implemented with a userspace proxy. This has since changed, and in the most common scenario, `kube-proxy` is simply manipulating `iptables` rules on every node. These rules redirect traffic that is destined for a Service IP to any one of the backing endpoint IPs. Since `kube-proxy` is a controller, it watches for state changes and reconciles to the appropriate state upon any modifications.

If we take a look at a `Service` that is already defined in our cluster, we can get a sense of how `kube-proxy` works behind the scenes:

```
$ kubectl get svc -n kube-system kubernetes-dashboard
NAME                   TYPE        CLUSTER-IP       EXTERNAL-IP   PORT(S)   AGE
kubernetes-dashboard   ClusterIP   10.104.154.139   <none>        443/TCP   40d
$ kubectl get ep -n kube-system kubernetes-dashboard
NAME                   ENDPOINTS                                    AGE
kubernetes-dashboard   192.168.63.200:8443,192.168.63.201:8443     40d
$ sudo iptables-save | grep KUBE | grep "kubernetes-dashboard"
-A KUBE-SEP-3HWS5OGCGRHMJ23K -s 192.168.63.201/32 -m comment --comment \
    "kube-system/kubernetes-dashboard:" -j KUBE-MARK-MASQ
-A KUBE-SEP-3HWS5OGCGRHMJ23K -p tcp -m comment --comment \
    "kube-system/kubernetes-dashboard:" -m tcp -j DNAT \
    --to-destination 192.168.63.201:8443
-A KUBE-SEP-XWHZMKM53W55IFOX -s 192.168.63.200/32 -m comment --comment \
    "kube-system/kubernetes-dashboard:" -j KUBE-MARK-MASQ
-A KUBE-SEP-XWHZMKM53W55IFOX -p tcp -m comment --comment \
    "kube-system/kubernetes-dashboard:" -m tcp -j DNAT \
    --to-destination 192.168.63.200:8443
-A KUBE-SERVICES ! -s 192.168.0.0/16 -d 10.104.154.139/32 -p tcp -m comment \
```

```
    --comment "kube-system/kubernetes-dashboard: cluster IP" -m tcp --dport 443 \
    -j KUBE-MARK-MASQ
-A KUBE-SERVICES -d 10.104.154.139/32 -p tcp -m comment --comment \
    "kube-system/kubernetes-dashboard: cluster IP" -m tcp --dport 443 \
    -j KUBE-SVC-XGLOHA7QRQ3V22RZ
-A KUBE-SVC-XGLOHA7QRQ3V22RZ -m comment --comment \
    "kube-system/kubernetes-dashboard:" -m statistic --mode random \
    --probability 0.50000000000 -j KUBE-SEP-XWHZMKM53W55IFOX
-A KUBE-SVC-XGLOHA7QRQ3V22RZ -m comment --comment \
    "kube-system/kubernetes-dashboard:" -j KUBE-SEP-3HWS5OGCGRHMJ23K
```

This might be a bit hard to follow, so let's break it down. In this scenario, we are looking at the kubernetes-dashboard ClusterIP Service. We see that it has a ClusterIP of 10.104.154.139 and Pod endpoints at 192.168.63.200:8443 and 192.168.63.201:8443. Here, kube-proxy has created a number of iptables rules to reflect this state on each node. These rules, in effect, say that any packets coming from the Pod CIDR (192.168.0.0/16) destined for the dashboard ClusterIP (10.104.154.139/32) on TCP port 443 should be redirected, randomly, to one of the downstream Pods hosting the dashboard container on container port 8443.

In this way, every Pod on every node is able to communicate with defined Services by way of the kube-proxy daemon's manipulation of iptables rules.

 iptables is the implementation most commonly found in the wild. With Kubernetes 1.9, a new IP Virtual Server (IPVS) implementation has been added. This is not only more performant but also affords a variety of load-balancing algorithms that may be utilized.

Service Discovery

In any environment where there is a high degree of dynamic process scheduling, we want a means by which to reliably discover where Service endpoints are located. This is true of many clustering technologies, and Kubernetes is no different. Fortunately, with the Service resource, we have a good place from which to enable Service discovery.

DNS

The most common way to discover Services within Kubernetes is via DNS. Although there are no native DNS controllers within the Kubernetes componentry itself, there are add-on controllers that may be utilized for providing DNS records for Service resources.

The two most widely deployed add-ons in this space are the kube-dns and CoreDNS controllers that are maintained by the community. These controllers watch the Pod and `Service` state from the API server and, in turn, automatically define a number of different DNS records. The difference between these two controllers is primarily implementation—the CoreDNS controller uses CoreDNS as its implementation, and kube-dns leverages dnsmasq.

Every `Service`, upon creation, gets a DNS A record associated with the virtual Service IP, which takes the form of `<service name>.<namespace>.svc.cluster.local`:

```
# kubectl get svc
NAME          TYPE        CLUSTER-IP    EXTERNAL-IP   PORT(S)    AGE
kubernetes    ClusterIP   10.96.0.1     <none>        443/TCP    35d
# kubectl run --image=alpine dns-test -it -- /bin/sh
If you don't see a command prompt, try pressing enter.
/ # nslookup kubernetes
Server:    10.96.0.10
Address 1: 10.96.0.10 kube-dns.kube-system.svc.cluster.local

Name:      kubernetes
Address 1: 10.96.0.1 kubernetes.default.svc.cluster.local
```

For headless `Services`, the records are slightly different:

```
# kubectl run --image=alpine headless-test -it -- /bin/sh
If you don't see a command prompt, try pressing enter.
/ # nslookup kube-headless
Name:      kube-headless
Address 1: 192.168.136.154 ip-192-168-136-154.ec2.internal
Address 2: 192.168.241.42 ip-192-168-241-42.ec2.internal
```

In this case, instead of an A record for the Service ClusterIP, users are presented with a list of A records that they may use at their discretion.

> *Headless* Services are ClusterIP Services with `clusterIP=None`. These are used when you would like to define a `Service` but do not require that it be managed by `kube-proxy`. Since you will still have access to the endpoints for the `Service`, you can leverage this if you would like to implement your own `Service` discovery mechanisms.

Environment Variables

In addition to DNS, a lesser-used feature but one to be aware of nonetheless is `Service` discovery using automatically injected environment variables. When a Pod is launched, a collection of variables describing the ClusterIP Services in the current namespace will be added to the process environment.

```
# kubectl get svc test
NAME    TYPE        CLUSTER-IP        EXTERNAL-IP   PORT(S)     AGE
test    ClusterIP   10.102.163.244    <none>        8080/TCP    9m
```

```
TEST_SERVICE_PORT_8080_8080=8080
TEST_SERVICE_HOST=10.102.163.244
TEST_PORT_8080_TCP_ADDR=10.102.163.244
TEST_PORT_8080_TCP_PORT=8080
TEST_PORT_8080_TCP_PROTO=tcp
TEST_SERVICE_PORT=8080
TEST_PORT=tcp://10.102.163.244:8080
TEST_PORT_8080_TCP=tcp://10.102.163.244:8080
```

This mechanism can be used in the absence of DNS capabilities, but there is one important caveat to keep in mind. Because the process environment is populated at Pod startup time, any Service discovery using this method requires that the necessary Service resources are defined *before* the Pod is. This method does not account for any updates to a Service after the Pod has been started.

Network Policy

A critical aspect of securing user workloads, whether with Kubernetes or not, involves ensuring that Services are only exposed to the appropriate consumers. If, for instance, you were developing an API that required a database backend, a typical deployment pattern would be to expose only the API endpoint to external consumers. Accessing the database would only be possible from the API Service itself. This type of Service isolation at layer 3 and layer 4 of the OSI model helps to ensure that the surface area for attack is limited. Traditionally, these types of restrictions have been implemented with some type of firewall, and, on Linux systems, this policy is typically enforced with IPTables.

IPTables rules, under normal circumstances, are only manipulated by a server administrator and are local to the node on which they are implemented. This poses a bit of a problem for Kubernetes users who would like to have self-service capabilities for securing their services.

Fortunately, Kubernetes provides the NetworkPolicy resource for users to define layer 3 and layer 4 rules as they pertain to their own workloads. The NetworkPolicy resource offers both ingress and egress rules that can be applied to namespaces, Pods, and even regular CIDR blocks.

Note that NetworkPolicy can only be defined in environments where the CNI plug-in supports this functionality. The Kubernetes API server will gladly accept your NetworkPolicy declaration, but since there is no controller to reconcile the declared state, no policies will be enacted. For instance, Flannel can provide an overlay network for Pod-to-Pod communication, but it does not include a policy agent. For this reason, many who want the functionality of Flannel's overlay with NetworkPolicy capabilities have turned to Canal, which combines the overlay of Flannel with the policy engine from Calico.

A typical NetworkPolicy manifest may look something like this:

```
apiVersion: networking.k8s.io/v1
kind: NetworkPolicy
metadata:
  name: backend-policy
  namespace: api-backend
spec:
  podSelector:
    matchLabels:
      role: db
  policyTypes:
  - Ingress
  - Egress
  ingress:
  - from:
    - namespaceSelector:
        matchLabels:
          project: api-midtier
    - podSelector:
        matchLabels:
          role: api-management
    ports:
    - protocol: TCP
      port: 3306
  egress:
  - to:
    - ipBlock:
        cidr: 10.3.4.5/32
    ports:
    - protocol: TCP
      port: 22
```

Reading and crafting these NetworkPolicy resources can take a bit of getting used to, but once you master the schema, this can be an extremely powerful tool at your disposal.

In this example, we are declaring a policy that will be placed on all Pods with the role=db labels in the api-backend Namespace. The ingress rules in place allow for traffic to port 3306 from either a Namespace with the `project=api-midtier` label or from a Pod with the `role=api-management` label. Additionally, we are limiting the outbound, or egress, traffic from the `role=db` Pods to an SSH server at 10.3.4.5. Perhaps we would use this for rsyncing backups to an externally available location.

Although these rules are relatively specific, we can also create broad allow-all or deny-all policies, for both ingress and egress traffic, for any given Namespace. For example, the following policy (and perhaps the most interesting) creates a default deny ingress policy for a Namespace:

```
apiVersion: networking.k8s.io/v1
kind: NetworkPolicy
metadata:
  name: default-deny
spec:
  podSelector: {}
  policyTypes:
  - Ingress
```

 It is important to note that, by default, there are no network restrictions for Pods. It is only through `NetworkPolicy` that we can begin to lock down Pod interconnectivity.

Service Mesh

Understanding the network flows between workloads can be a complicated endeavor. In the simplest of cases, a single Pod replica with a single container is fronted by a `Service` resource. With this scenario, we simply need to analyze where traffic is originating from by looking at the container's application logs.

In a microservices environment, however, it is often typical for traffic to enter the cluster via an Ingress, which is backed by a `Service`, which is then backed by any number of Pod replicas. Further, these Pods might, themselves, connect to other cluster `Service`s and their respective backing Pods. As you can probably see, these flows get intricate very quickly, and this is where service mesh solutions may help.

A service mesh is simply a collection of "smart" proxies that can help users with a variety of east-west or Pod-to-Pod networking needs. These proxies may operate as sidecar containers in the application Pods or may operate as `DaemonSet`s, where they are node-local infrastructure components that may be utilized by any of the Pods on a given node. Simply configure your Pods to proxy their traffic to these service mesh proxies (typically with environment variables), and your Pods are now a part of the mesh.

Whether you deploy as a sidecar or as a `DaemonSet` is typically determined by the service mesh technology that you choose and/or the availability of resources on your cluster. Since these proxies run as Pods, they do consume cluster resources and, as such, you need to make decisions about whether these resources should be shared or associated with a Pod.

Service mesh solutions typically provide common functionality.

Traffic management
> Most service mesh solutions include some features targeted at driving incoming requests at particular `Services`. This can enable advanced patterns such as canary and blue/green deployments. Additionally, some solutions are protocol-aware. Instead of acting as a "dumb" layer 4 proxy, they have the ability to introspect higher-level protocols and make intelligent proxying decisions. For example, if a particular upstream were to respond slowly to HTTP requests, the proxy could weight that backend lower than a responsive upstream.

Observability
> When deploying microservices to a Kubernetes cluster, the interconnectivity between Pods can quickly become difficult to understand. As more and more Pods communicate with one another, how should you debug a user-reported connectivity issue? How do you find the application that is slow to respond? Most service mesh solutions provide automatic mechanisms for distributed tracing (commonly based on the OpenTracing standard). In a transparent way, you can uniquely trace the flow of individual requests.

Security
> In environments where the underlying network provides no default encryption (which is common for most CNI plug-ins), service mesh can intercede by offering mutual TLS for all east-west traffic. This can be advantageous because policies may be enforced such that all connectivity is secure by default.

Projects like Istio (*https://istio.io*), Linkerd (*https://linkerd.io*), and Conduit (*https://conduit.io*) are commonly utilized service mesh solutions. If the features just mentioned speak to your use case, give these projects some consideration.

Summary

Networking in any distributed system is always complex. Kubernetes simplifies this critical capability by offering well-conceived abstractions over multiple layers of the OSI networking stack. Often, these abstractions are implemented with tried and tested networking technologies that have been reliably utilized for decades. However, because these abstractions are intended to provide a common interface for functionality, you, as the cluster administrator, are free to utilize the implementations that best suit your needs. When coupling your application's networking requirements with its deployment manifests, it is much easier to deploy complex, stable, and secure application architectures.

## CHAPTER 11

Monitoring Kubernetes

It's all well and good to set up or use a Kubernetes cluster from a public cloud vendor. But without the right strategy for monitoring metrics and logs from that cluster and firing appropriate alerts when something goes wrong, the cluster that you have created is a disaster waiting to happen. Although Kubernetes makes it easy for developers to build and deploy their applications, it also creates applications that are dependent on Kubernetes for successful operation. This means that, when a cluster fails, your users' applications often fail, as well. And, if a cluster fails too often, users lose trust in the system and begin to question the value of the cluster and its operators. This chapter discusses approaches to developing and deploying monitoring and alerting for your Kubernetes cluster to prevent this from happening. Additionally, we describe how you can add monitoring onto your cluster so that application developers can automatically take advantage of it for their own applications.

Goals for Monitoring

Before we step into the details of how to monitor your cluster, it's important to go over the goals for this monitoring. All of the specifics of how to deploy and manage monitoring are in service of these goals, and thus a crystal clear sense of the *why?* will help in understanding the *what*.

Obviously, the first and foremost goal of monitoring is reliability. In this case, reliability is both that of the Kubernetes cluster and that of the applications running on top of the cluster. As an example of this relationship, consider a binary, like the controller manager. If it stops operating correctly, service discovery will start to slowly go out of date. Existing Services will have already been properly propogated to the DNS server in the cluster, but new Services, or Services that change due to rollouts or scaling operations, won't have their DNS updated.

This failure shows the importance of understanding the underlying Kubernetes architecture. If you can't crisply explain the role of the controller manager in the overall Kubernetes cluster, this might be a good time to step back and review Chapter 3, which covers Kubernetes components and architecture.

This sort of failure actually won't be reflected in the correct operation of the Kubernetes cluster itself. All of its `Service` discovery is largely static after cluster initialization. However, it is reflected in the correctness of the applications running on top of the Kubernetes cluster, since their `Service` discovery and failover will themselves start failing.

This example demonstrates two important points about Kubernetes monitoring. The first is that, in many cases, the cluster itself appears to be operating correctly, but it is actual failing. This points to the importance of not just monitoring the cluster pieces but also monitoring the cluster functionality that users require. In this case, the best type of monitoring would be a blackbox monitor that continuously deploys a new Pod and `Service` and that validates that the `Service` discovery works as expected.

 Throughout this chapter, we refer to two different types of monitoring. *Whitebox* monitoring looks at signals that applications produce and uses these signals to find problems. *Blackbox* or *probe* monitoring uses the public interfaces (e.g., Kubernetes) to take actions with known expected outcomes (e.g., "Create a `ReplicaSet` of size three leads to three pods") and fires alerts if the expected outcome does not occur.

The other important lesson of this DNS example is how important it is to have proper alerting in place. If you only notice that there is a problem with your Kubernetes cluster when you have users complaining about failures of their application, you have a monitoring gap. Although live site incidents are an inevitable part of running a `Service`, customer-reported incidents should be nonexistent in a well-monitored system.

In addition to reliability, another significant feature of a monitoring system is providing observability into your Kubernetes cluster. There are lots of reasons why observing your cluster is important and relevant.

It is one thing to be able to fire monitoring alerts that indicate that there is a problem with your cluster. It is another to be able to determine exactly what is going wrong to cause the alert, and yet another to be able to see and correct problems before they become end-user facing problems. The ability to observe, visualize, and query your monitoring data is a critical tool in determining what problems are happening and in identifying problems before they become incidents.

In addition to insight in the service of reliability, another important use case for cluster monitoring data is that of providing users with insight into the operation of the cluster. For example, users may be curious to know, on average, how long it takes to pull and begin running their images. A user may be wondering how fast, in practice, a Kubernetes DNS record is created, or a person from finance may want to track whether users are really using all of the compute resources they are requesting. All of this information is available from a cluster monitoring system.

Differences Between Logging and Monitoring

One important topic to cover before we delve into the details of monitoring Kubernetes is the difference between *logging* and *monitoring*. Though closely related, they are actually quite different and are used for different problems and often stored in different infrastructure.

Logging records events (e.g., a Pod being created or an API call failing), and monitoring records statistics (e.g., the latency of a particular request, the CPU used by a process, or the number of requests to a particular endpoint). Logged records, by their nature, are discrete, whereas monitoring data is a sampling of some continuous value.

Logging systems are generally used to search for relevant information. ("Why did creating that Pod fail?" "Why didn't that Service work correctly?") For this reason, log storage systems are oriented around storing and querying vast quantities of data, whereas monitoring systems are generally geared around visualization. ("Show me the CPU usage over the last hour.") Thus, they are stored in systems that can efficiently store time-series data.

It is worth noting that neither logging nor monitoring alone are sufficient to understand your cluster. Monitoring data can give you a good sense of the overall health of your cluster and can help you identify anomalous events that may be occuring. Logging, on the other hand, is critical for diving in and understanding what is actually happening, possibly across many machines, to cause such anomalous behavior.

Building a Monitoring Stack

Now that you have some understanding of why and what you may need to monitor your Kubernetes cluster, let's take a look at how you might accomplish it.

Getting Data from Your Cluster and Applications

Monitoring begins with exposing data to the monitoring system. Some of this data is obtained generically from the kernel about the cgroups and namespaces that make up containers in your cluster, but the bulk of the information that is useful to monitor is added to the applications themselves by the developer. There are numerous different ways to integrate metrics into your application, but one of the most popular—and the choice of Kuberentes for exposing metrics—is the Prometheus monitoring interface (*https://prometheus.io*).

Every server in Kubernetes exposes monitoring data via an HTTP(S) endpoint that serves the monitored data using the Prometheus protocol. If you have a Kubernetes kubelet server that is up and running, you can access this data via a standard HTTP client, like `curl`, at the following URL: *http://localhost:9093*.

To integrate new application metrics into your code, you need to link in the relevant Prometheus libraries. This not only adds the right HTTP server to your application but also exposes the specific metrics for scraping from that server. Prometheus has official libraries for Go, Java, Python, and Ruby, in addition to unofficial libraries for numerous other languages.

Here's an example of how to instrument a Go application. First, you add the Prometheus server to your code:

```
import "github.com/prometheus/client_golang/prometheus/promhttp"
...
func main() {
...
    http.Handle("/metrics", promhttp.Handler())
...
}
```

Once you have the server running, you need to define a metric and observe values:

```
"github.com/prometheus/client_golang/prometheus"
...
    histogram := prometheus.NewHistogram(...)
...
    histogram.Observe(someLatency)
...
```

In addition to the monitoring information that Kubernetes makes available, each of the Kubernetes binaries logs a great deal of information to the `stdout` file stream. Often, this output is captured and redirected to a log-rotated file, such as */var/lib/kubernetes-apiserver.log*. If you SSH into the master node running the Kubernetes API server, you can find the API server log file in */var/lib/kube-apiserver.log*, and you can watch the log lines in action using the `tail -f ...` command. The Kubernetes components use the *github.com/google/glog* library to log data to the file at different severity levels. When looking through the file, you can detect these severity levels by looking at the first letter that was logged. For example, an error-level log looks like:

```
E0610 03:39:40.323732    1753 reflector.go:205] ...
```

You can see the *E* for the error log level, the time of the log, and the file that logged.

The Kubernetes components also log data at different levels of verbosity. Most installations of Kubernetes set the verbosity at two, which is also the default. This produces a good balance between verbosity and spam. If you need to increase or decrease the verbosity of the logging, you can use the `--v` flag and set it between 0 and 10, where 10 indicates maximum verbosity, which can be quite spammy. You can also use the `-vmodule` flag to set the verbosity for a particular file or set of files.

 Setting the verbosity of your logs to a higher level increases visibilty, but it comes at a price—both financially and in terms of performance. Because the absolute number of logs is higher, it increases storage and retention costs and can make your querying slower. When increasing the logging level, generally only do it for a short period of time and be sure that you bring the logging back to a standard level as soon as possible.

Aggregating Metrics and Logs from Multiple Sources

Once you have your components generating data, you need a place to group it together or to aggregate it and then, after it is aggregated, store it for querying and introspection. This section deals with aggregation of logging and monitoring data, and later sections deal with choices in terms of storage.

When it comes to aggregation, there are two different styles. In *pull aggregation*, the aggregation system proactively reaches out to each monitored system and pulls the monitoring information into the aggregate store. An alternate approach is a *push-based monitoring system*, in which the system that is being monitored is responsible for sending its metrics to the aggregation system. Each of these two different monitoring designs has advantages and disadvantages and are easier or harder to implement, depending on the details of the system. When you look at Prometheus and Fluentd, the two systems that we examine in detail for logging and monitoring aggregation, you can see that the two systems have different designs. Getting to know each of them and why they chose their designs helps you understand the trade-offs.

Prometheus is a pull-based aggregator for monitoring metrics. As we have seen, when you expose a Prometheus metric, it is exposed as a web page that can be scraped and aggregated into the Prometheus server. Prometheus chooses this design because it makes adding more systems to monitor quite trivial. As long as the system implements the expected interface, it is as simple as adding an additional URL to the Prometheus configuration, and that server's data will start being monitored. Because Prometheus is responsible for scraping the data and aggregating it at its own pace, the Prometheus system doesn't need to worry about bursty or lagging clients sending it data at different intervals. Instead, Prometheus always knows exactly what time it is when it requests the monitoring data, and it also is in control of the rate at which it samples data, ensuring that the sample rate is consistent and evenly distributed across all systems being monitored.

In contrast, the `fluentd` daemon (*https://www.fluentd.org*) is a push-based log aggregator. Just as Prometheus chose the pull model for a variety of pragmatic reasons, Fluentd chose the push model based on a number of real design considerations. The primary reason that Fluentd selected a push-based model is that nearly every system that logs does so to a file or to a stream on the local machine. As a result, to integrate into the logging stack, Fluentd needs to read from a large variety of files on disk to get the latest logs. It is generally not very possible to inject custom code into the system being monitored (e.g., to print to a logging system instead of `stdout`). Consequently, Fluentd chose to take control of the logging information, read it from each of the different files, and push it into an aggregate log system, which means that adding `fluentd` to an existing binary is quite straightforward. You don't change the binary at all. Instead, you configure `fluentd` to load in data from a file in a specific path and to forward those logs to a log storage system. To illustrate this, here is an example Fluentd configuration to monitor and push Kubernetes API server audit logs:

```
<source>
      @type tail
      format json
      path /var/log/audit
      pos_file /var/log/audit.pos
      tag audit
      time_key time
      time_format %Y-%m-%dT%H:%M:%S.%N%z
</source>
….
```

You can see from this example that Fluentd is highly configurable, taking the file location, the file format, and expressions for both parsing dates from the logs and adding tags to the data. Because the Kubernetes servers use the `glog` package, log lines follow a consistent format, thus you can expect (and extract) structured data from every line that Kubernetes logs.

 Prometheus is often linked into an application, but you can still use it with off-the-shelf software. There are a wide variety of Prometheus adapters that can be run as sidecars next to your application. These can be ambassadors between the application and the expected Prometheus interfaces. In many cases (e.g., Redis or Java), the adapter knows directly how to talk to the application to expose its data in a format that Prometheus can understand. Additionally, there are adapters from common monitoring protocols (e.g., StatsD) such that Prometheus can also scrape metrics that were originally intended for some other system.

Storing Data for Retrieval and Querying

After monitoring and logging data has been aggregated by Prometheus or Fluentd, the data still needs to be stored somewhere for retention for a period of time. How long you retain monitoring data depends on the needs of your system and the costs you're willing to pay, in terms of storage space for the data. However, in our experience, the minimum you should have is 30–45 days' worth of data. At first, this might seem like a lot, but the truth is that many problems begin slowly and take a long time before they become apparent. Having a historical perspective allows you to see differences before they became significant problems and to more easily identify the source of the problem.

For example, a release four weeks ago could have introduced some additional latency in request processing. That might not have been significant enough to cause problems, but when combined with a more recent increase in request traffic, requests are being processed far too slowly and your alerts are firing. Without historical data to pinpoint the initial increase in latency four weeks ago, you wouldn't be able to identify the release (and thus the changes) that caused the problem. You would be stuck searching through the code looking for the issue, which can take significantly longer.

As with aggregators, there are a number of choices for storing monitoring and logging data. Many of the storage options run as cloud services. These can be good options, since they eliminate operations for the storage part of your cluster, but there are also good reasons for running your own storage, siuch as being able to precisely control data location and retention. Even in the space of open source storage for logging and monitoring, you have multiple choices. In the interests of time and space, we discuss two of them here: InfluxDB for maintaining time series data and Elasticsearch for storing log-structured data.

InfluxDB

InfluxDB is a time series database that is capable of storing large amounts of data in a compact and searchable format. It is an open source project that is freely available for a variety of operating systems. InfluxDB is distributed as a binary package (*https://portal.influxdata.com/downloads#influxdb*) that can easily be installed.

 A *time series* is a collection of data pairs, in which one member is a value and the other is an instant in time. For example, you might have a time series that represents the CPU usage of a process over time. Each pair would combine the CPU usage and the instant at which that CPU usage was observed.

One important question when running InfluxDB is whether to run it as a container on the Kubernetes cluster itself. In general, this is not a recommended setup. You are using InfluxDB to monitor the cluster, so you want monitoring data to continue to be accessible, even if the cluster itself is having problems.

Elasticsearch

Elasticsearch is a system for ingesting and searching log-based data. Unlike InfluxDB, which is oriented toward storing time series data, Elasticsearch is designed to ingest large quantities of unstructured or semistructured log files and to make them available via a search interface. Elasticsearch can be installed from binary packages (*https://www.elastic.co/downloads/elasticsearch*).

Visualizing and Interacting with Your Data

Of course, storing the information isn't very useful if you can't then access it in interesting ways to analyze and understand what is going on in your system. To that end, visualization is a critical component in a complete monitoring stack. Visualization is different for logging and metric data. Metric monitoring data is generally visualized as graphs, either as a time series that shows a few metrics over time, or as a histogram that summarizes the statistics for a value across a time window. Sometimes it is visualized as an aggregate across a window of time (e.g., the sum of all errors each hour for a week). One of the most popular interfaces for visualizing metrics is the open source Grafana dashboard (*https://grafana.com*), which can interface with Prometheus and other metric sources and can enable you to build your own dashboards or to import dashboards created by other users.

For logged data, the search interface is more oriented around ad hoc queries and exploration of the data that has been logged. One of the popular interfaces for viewing logging data is the Kibana web frontend (*https://www.elastic.co/products/kibana*), which allows you to search, browse, and introspect data that has been logged to Elasticsearch.

What to Monitor?

Now that you have assembled your monitoring stack, there are still two important questions left unanswered: what to monitor and, correspondingly, what to alert on?

When assembling monitoring information, as with nearly all software, it is valuable to take a layered approach. The layers to monitor are machines, cluster basics, cluster add-ons, and finally, user applications. In this way, beginning with the basics, each layer in the monitoring stack builds on top of the layer below it. When built like this, identifying a problem is an exercise in diving down through the layers until the cause is identified. However, correspondingly if a healthy layer is reached (e.g., all of the machines in the cluster appear to be operating correctly), it becomes obvious that the problem lies in the layer above (e.g., the cluster infrastructure).

The monitoring that was described in the previous paragraph was all *whitebox monitoring*, by which we mean that the monitoring was based upon detailed knowledge of the system and how it is assembled. Each part of the system is monitored for deviations from the expected, and such deviations are reported.

The contrast to whitebox monitoring is *blackbox* or *prober-based monitoring*. In blackbox monitoring, you don't assume or know any details of how the system is constructed. Instead, you simply consume the external interface, like a customer or user would, and observe whether your actions have the expected results. For example, a simple prober for a Kubernetes cluster might schedule a Pod onto the cluster and verify that the Pod was successfully created and the application running in the Pod (e.g., nginx) can be reached via a Kubernetes Service. If a blackbox monitor succeeds, it can generally be assumed that the system is healthy. If the blackbox fails, the system is not.

The value of blackbox monitoring is that it gives you a very clear signal about the health of your system. The downside is that it gives you very little visibility into *why* your system has failed. Consequently, it is essential to combine both whitebox and blackbox monitoring to have a robust, useful monitoring system.

Monitoring Machines

The machines (physical or virtual) that make up your cluster are the foundation of your Kubernetes cluster. If the machines in your cluster are overloaded or misbehaving, all other operations within the cluster are suspect. Monitoring the machines is essential to understanding whether your basic infrastructure is operating correctly.

Fortunately, monitoring machine metrics with Prometheus is quite straightforward. The Prometheus project has a node exporter daemon (*https://github.com/prometheus/node_exporter*), which can run on each machine and which exposes basic information gathered from the kernel and other system sources so that Prometheus can scrape. This data includes:

- CPU usage
- Network usage
- Disk usage and free space available
- Memory usage
- …and much more

You can download the node exporter from GitHub, or build it yourself. When you have the node exporter binary in your system, you can set it to run automatically as a daemon using this simple *systemd* unit file:

```
[Unit]
Description=Node Exporter

[Service]
User=node_exporter
EnvironmentFile=/etc/sysconfig/node_exporter
ExecStart=/usr/sbin/node_exporter $OPTIONS

[Install]
WantedBy=multi-user.target
```

After you have the *node exporter* up and running, you can configure Prometheus to scrape metrics from each machine in your cluster, using the following scrape configuration in Prometheus:

```
- job_name: "node"
  scrape_interval: "60s"
  static_configs:
  - targets:
    - 'server.1:9100'
    - 'server.2:9100'
    - ...
    - 'server.N:9100'
```

Monitoring Kubernetes

Fortunately, all of the pieces of the Kubernetes infrastructure expose metrics using the Prometheus API, and there is also a Kubernetes `Service` discovery that you can use to automatically discover and monitor the Kubernetes components in your cluster:

```
- job_name: 'kubernetes-apiservers'
  kubernetes_sd_configs:
  - role: endpoints
  ....
```

You can reuse this `Service` discovery implementation to add scraping for multiple different components in the cluster, like the API servers and the kubelets.

Monitoring Applications

Finally, you can also use the Kubernetes `Service` discovery to find and scrape metrics from Pods themselves. This means that you automatically scrape metrics from pieces of the Kubernetes cluster designed to run as Pods (e.g., the kube-dns servers), and you automatically scrape all metrics from Pods that are run by users, assuming, that is, that the users integrate and expose Prometheus-compatible metrics. However, after your users see how easy it is to get automated metric monitoring via Prometheus, they are unlikely to use any other monitoring.

Blackbox Monitoring

As mentioned earlier, blackbox monitoring probes the external API of the system, ensuring that it responds correctly. In this case, the external API of the system is the Kubernetes API. Probing of the system can be performed by an agent that makes calls against the Kubernetes API. It is a challenge to determine whether this agent runs inside the Kubernetes cluster. Running it inside the cluster makes it significantly easier to manage, but it also makes it vulnerable to cluster failures. If you choose to monitor the cluster from within the cluster, it is essential to also have a "watchdog alert" that fires if a prober hasn't been run to completion in the previous N minutes. There are many different blackbox tests you can design for the Kubernetes API.

As a simple example, you can imagine writing a small script:

```
#!/bin/bash

# exit on all failures
set -e

NAMESPACE=blackbox

# tear down the namespace no matter what
function teardown {
  kubectl delete namespace ${NAMESPACE}
}
trap teardown ERR

# Create a probe namespace
kubectl create namespace ${NAMESPACE}
kubectl create -f my-deployment-spec.yaml

# Test connectivity to your app here, wget etc.

teardown
```

You could run this script every five minutes (or some other interval) to validate that the cluster was working properly. A more complete example might be to write an application that continuously tests the Kubernetes API, similar to the previous script, but also export Prometheus metrics so you can scrape the blackbox monitoring data into Prometheus.

Ultimately, the limits of what you blackbox test are really the limits of your imagination and your willingness to design and build tests. As of this writing, there are no good off-the-shelf blackbox probers for the Kubernetes API. It's up to you to design and build such tests.

Streaming Logs

In addition to all of the metric monitoring data, it's also important to get the logs from your cluster. This includes things like the kubelet logs from each node, as well as the API server, scheduler, and controller manager logs from the master. These are generally located in */var/log/kube-*.log*. You can set them up for export with a simple Fluentd configuration like:

```
<source>
  @type tail
  path /var/log/kube-apiserver.log
  pos_file /var/log/fluentd-kube-apiserver.log.pos
  tag kube-apiserver
  ...
</source>
```

It is also useful to log anything that a container running in the cluster writes to stdout. By default, Docker writes all of the logs from the containers to */var/log/containers/*.log*, and thus you can use that expression in a similar Fluentd configuration to also export log data for all containers that run in the cluster.

Alerting

After you have monitoring working correctly, it's time to add alerts. Defining and implementing alerts in Prometheus or other systems is beyond the scope of this book. If you have never done monitoring before, we strongly recommend obtaining a book dedicated to the subject.

However, when it comes to which alerts to define, there are two philosophies to consider. The first, similar to whitebox monitoring, is to alert when signals stop being nominal. For example, to understand how much CPU an API server normally consumes, and alert if the CPU usage of an API server goes out of that range.

The benefits of this approach to monitoring are that you frequently notice problems before they are user impacting. Systems start to behave strangely or poorly often long before they have catastrophic failures.

The downside of this alerting strategy is that it can be quite noisy. Signals, like CPU usage, can be quite varied, and alerting when things change—even though there may not necessarily be a real problem—can lead to tired, frustrated operators, who ignore pages when there are real alerts.

The alternate monitoring strategy, more similar to blackbox monitoring, is to alert on the signals that your user sees. For example, the latency of a request to the API server or the number of 403 (Unauthorized) responses that your API server is returning. The benefit of this alerting is that, by definition, there can't be a noisy alert. Every time such an alert fires, there is a real problem. The downside of such alerting is that you do not notice problems until they are customer facing.

Like everything, the best path for alerting lies with a balance of each. For signals that you understand very well, which have stable values, whitebox alerting offers a critical heads-up before significant problems occur. Blackbox alerting, on the other hand, gives you high-quality alerts caused by real, user-facing problems. A successful alerting strategy combines both styles of alerts (and, perhaps more critically, adapts these alerts) as your understanding of your particular clusters grows.

Summary

Logging and monitoring are critical components of understanding how your cluster and your applications are performing, and/or where they are having problems. Constructing a high-quality alerting and monitoring stack should be one of the very first priorities after a cluster is successfully set up. Done correctly, a logging and monitoring stack that is automatically available to the users of a Kubernetes cluster is a key differentiator that makes it feasible for developers to deploy and manage reliable applications at scale.

## CHAPTER 12

Disaster Recovery

If you're like most users, you have probably looked to Kubernetes, at least in part, for its ability to automatically recover from failure. And, of course, Kubernetes does a great job of keeping your workloads up and running. However, as with any complex system, there is always room for failure. Whether that failure is due to something like hardware fault on a node, or even data loss on the etcd cluster, we want to have systems in place to ensure that we can recover in a timely and reliable fashion.

High Availability

A first principle in any disaster recovery strategy is to design your systems to minimize the possibility of failure in the first place. Naturally, designing a foolproof system is an impossibility, but we should always build with the worst-case scenarios in mind.

When building production-grade Kubernetes clusters, best practices always dictate that critical components are highly available. In some cases, as with the API server, these may have an active-active configuration, whereas with items like the scheduler and controller manager, these operate in an active-passive manner. When these control plane surfaces are deployed properly, a user should not notice that a failure has even occurred.

Similarly, we recommend that your etcd backing store is deployed in a three- or five-node cluster configuration. You may certainly deploy larger clusters (always with an odd number of members), but clusters of this size should suffice for the vast majority of use cases. The failure tolerance of the etcd cluster increases with the number of members that are present: one-node failure tolerance for a three-node cluster, and a two-node tolerance for a five-node cluster. However, as the size of the etcd cluster increases, the performance of the cluster may slowly degrade. When choosing your cluster size, always be sure that you are well within your expected etcd load.

 Understand that a failure of the Kubernetes control plane typically does not affect the data plane. In other words, if your API server, controller manager, or scheduler fails, your Pods will often continue to operate as they are. In most scenarios, you simply are not able to effect change on the cluster until the control plane is brought back online.

State

The question at the center of every disaster recovery solution is, "How do I restore to a well-defined previous state?" We want to be sure that, when disaster strikes, we have copies of all of the data that we need to return to an operational state.

Fortunately, with Kubernetes, most of the cluster's operational state is centrally located in the etcd cluster. Therefore, we spend a good deal of time ensuring that we can reconstitute its contents, should a failure occur.

But etcd is not the only state that we care about. We also need to be sure that we have backups of some of the static assets created (or, in some cases, provided) during deployment. The following are the items that should be safely tucked away:

All PKI assets used by the Kubernetes API server
These are typically located in the */etc/kubernetes/pki* directory.

Any Secret encryption keys
These keys are stored in a static file that is specified with the `--experimental-encryption-provider-config` in the API server parameter. If these keys are lost, any Secret data is not recoverable.

Any administrator credentials
Most deployment tools (including `kubeadm`) create static administrator credentials and provide them in a `kubeconfig` file. Although these may be recreated, securely storing them off-cluster might reduce recovery time.

Application Data

In addition to all of the state necessary to reconstitute Kubernetes itself, recovering stateful Pods would be useless unless we also recovered any persistent data associated with those Pods.

Persistent Volumes

There are a variety of ways that a user may persist data from within Kubernetes. How you back this data up is contingent on your environment.

For instance, in a cloud provider, it may be as simple as reattaching any persistent volumes to their respective Pods, with the working assumption that your Kubernetes failure is unrelated to the availability of persistent volumes. You might also rely on the underlying architecture backing the volumes themselves. For instance, with Ceph-based volumes, having multiple replicas of your data may be enough.

The way that you implement the backup of application data depends heavily on the implementation that you have chosen for how volumes are presented to Kubernetes. Keep this in mind, as you develop a wider disaster recovery strategy.

> Kubernetes does not currently have a mechanism for defining volume snapshots, but this is a feature that seems to be getting traction in recent community conversations.

Local Data

One often-overlooked aspect of data backup is that users sometimes unknowingly persist critical data to a node's local disk. This is particularly common in on-premises environments, where network-attached storage may not always be present. Without appropriate guardrails in place (e.g., PodSecurityPolicys and/or more generic admission controllers), users might make use of emptyDir or hostPath volumes, possibly holding incorrect assumptions about the longevity of this data.

> Recall our discussion about admission control in Chapter 7. If you would like to enforce restrictions on local disk access, these may be implemented with PodSecurityPolicys, primarily with the vol umes and allowedHostPaths controls.

It may not even be a failure scenario where this issue is encountered. Because worker nodes are widely considered to be ephemeral in nature, even a planned maintenance or retirement of a node may yield a poor experience for your users. Always be sure to have the appropriate controls in place.

Worker Nodes

We can think of worker nodes as being replaceable. When designing our disaster recovery strategy for worker nodes, we simply need to have a process in place whereby we can reliably recreate a worker node. If you have deployed Kubernetes to a cloud provider, the task is often as simple as launching a new instance and joining that worker to the control plane. In bare-metal environments (or those without API-directed infrastructure), this process may be a bit more onerous, but it will be mostly identical.

In the event that you are able to identify that a node is approaching failure, or in cases where you need to perform maintenance, Kubernetes offers two commands that may be of assistance.

First, and particularly important in high-churn clusters, `kubectl cordon` renders a node unschedulable. This can help stem the tide of new Pods affecting our ability to perform a recovery action on a worker node. Second, the `kubectl drain` command allows us to remove and reschedule all running Pods from a target node. This is useful in scenarios where we intend to remove a node from the cluster.

etcd

Because an etcd cluster retains multiple replicas of its dataset, complete failure is relatively rare. However, backing up etcd is always considered a best practice for production clusters.

Just as with any other database, etcd stores its data on disk, and with that comes a variety of ways that we can back up that data. At the lowest levels, we can use block and filesystem snapshots, and this might work well. However, there is a significant amount of coordination that needs to take place when attempting the backup. In both cases, you need to be sure that etcd has been quiesced, typically by stopping the etcd process on the etcd member where you intend to perform the backup. Further, to ensure that all in-flight data has been saved, you need to be sure to first freeze the underlying filesystem. As you can see, this can become pretty cumbersome.

This technique may start to make sense with network-attached block devices that are backing etcd. Many clusters that are built in public cloud environments choose to use this technique because it shortens the time to recovery. Instead of replacing the data on disk with a backup, these users simply reattach the existing etcd data volumes to the new etcd member nodes, and, fingers crossed, are back in business. While this solution may work, there are a number of reasons why it may be less than ideal. Chief among them are concerns surrounding data consistency, since this approach is relatively difficult to perform correctly.

The most common approach, albeit resulting in slightly longer recovery times, is to utilize the native etcd command-line tools:

```
ETCDCTL_API=3 etcdctl --endpoints $ENDPOINT snapshot save etcd-`date +%Y%m%d`.db
```

This can be run against an active etcd member, and the resulting file should be offloaded from the cluster and stored in a reliable location, such as an object store.

In the event that you need to restore, you simply need to execute the aptly named `restore` command:

```
ETCDCTL_API=3 etcdctl snapshot restore etcd-$DATE.db --name $MEMBERNAME
```

Do this against each of the replacement members of a new cluster.

Although all of these backup strategies are viable, there are important caveats to consider.

First, when backing up by either method, be cognizant of the fact that you are backing up the entire etcd keyspace. It is a complete copy of the state of etcd at the time of backup. Although our goal is typically to create a carbon copy, there may be scenarios in which we may not actually want the entire backup. Perhaps we simply want to bring the production Namespace up in an expeditious manner. With this type of recovery, we are restoring indiscriminately.

Second, just as with any type of database backup, if the consuming application (in our case, Kubernetes itself) is not quiesced during backup, there may be transient state that has not been consistently applied to the backing store. The likelihood of this being highly problematic is small but is present nonetheless.

And finally, if you have enabled any Kubernetes Aggregate API servers or have used an etcd-backed Calico implementation (both of which use their own etcd instances), these would not be backed up if you have only targeted the cluster's primary etcd endpoints. You would need to develop additional strategies to capture and restore that data.

 If you are using a managed Kubernetes offering, you may not have direct access to etcd or even to the disks that are backing etcd. In this case, you need to utilize a different backup and restore methodology.

Ark

A purpose-built tool that is widely used for backup and recovery of Kubernetes clusters is Ark, from Heptio (*https://github.com/heptio/ark*). This tool is not only concerned with the management of Kubernetes resource data but also serves as a framework for managing application data.

What makes Ark different from the methods we have already described is that it is Kubernetes aware. Instead of blindly backing up etcd data, Ark performs backups by way of the Kubernetes API itself. This ensures that the data is always consistent, and it allows for more selective backup strategies. Let's consider a few examples.

Partial backup and restore

Because Ark is Kubernetes-aware, it is able to facilitate more advanced backup strategies. For instance, if you were interested in backing up only production workloads, you could use a simple label selector:

```
ark backup create prod-backup --selector env=prod
```

This would back up all resources with the label env=prod.

Restoration to a new environment

Ark is capable of restoring backup to an entirely new cluster or even to a new Namespace within an existing cluster. Beyond the topic of disaster recovery, this may also be used to facilitate interesting testing scenarios.

Partial restoration

In the midst of downtime, it is often preferable to restore the most critical systems first. With partial restoration, Ark allows you to prioritize which resources are restored.

Persistent data backup

Ark is able to integrate with a variety of cloud providers to automatically snapshot persistent volumes. Additionally, it includes a hook mechanism for performing actions, such as filesystem freezing prior to and after the snapshot has been taken.

Scheduled backups

With an on-cluster service managing state, Ark is capable of scheduling backups. This can be particularly useful for ensuring that backups are taken regularly.

Off-cluster backups

Ark integrates with various S3-compatible object storage solutions. Although these solutions may be run on a cluster, it is advisable to offload these backups so that they are available in the event of failure.

You likely will not need all of these features, but with the wide degree of freedom that Ark offers, you can choose the pieces that make sense for your backup solution.

Summary

When devising a disaster recovery strategy for your Kubernetes cluster, there are many areas to consider. How you design this strategy depends on your selections for complementary technologies, as well as the details of your particular use case. As you build this muscle, be sure to regularly exercise your ability to completely restore your production systems with fully automated solutions. This not only prepares you for failure but also helps you think about your deployment strategy more holistically. Of course, we hope you never need to use the techniques just outlined. But should the need arise, you will be better off for having considered these cases upfront.

## CHAPTER 13

Extending Kubernetes

Kubernetes has a rich API that provides much of the functionality that you might need to build and operate a distributed system. However, the API is purposefully generic, aimed at the 80% use cases. Taking advantage of the rich ecosystem of add-ons and extensions that exist for Kubernetes can add significant new functionality and enable new experiences for users of your cluster. You may even choose to implement your own custom add-ons and extensions that are suited to the particular needs of your company or environment.

Kubernetes Extension Points

There are a number of different ways to extend a Kubernetes cluster, and each offers a different set of capabilities and additional operational complexity. The following sections describe these various extension points in detail and provide insight into how they can extend the functionality of a cluster and into the additional operational requirements of these extensions.

The four types of extensibility are:

- Cluster daemons for automation
- Cluster assistants for extended functionality
- Extending the life cycle of the API server
- Adding more APIs

The truth, of course, about some of these classifications is that they are somewhat arbitrary, and there are different extensions that can combine multiple kinds of extensibility to provide additional functionality for a cluster. The categories described here are intended to help guide your discussion and planning for extending a Kubernetes cluster. They are guidelines—not hard and fast rules.

Cluster Daemons

The simplest and most common form of cluster extensibility is the cluster daemon. Just like a daemon or agent running on a single machine adds automation (e.g., log rolling) to a single machine, a cluster daemon adds automation functionality to a cluster. Cluster daemons have two definiing characteristics. The agent needs to run on the Kubernetes cluster itself, and the agent needs to add functionality to the cluster that is automatically provided to all users of the cluster without any action on their part.

To be able to deploy a cluster daemon onto the Kubernetes cluster it helps manage, the cluster daemon itself is packaged as a container image. It is then configured via Kubernetes configuration objects and run on the cluster either via a `DaemonSet` or a `Deployment`. Typically, these cluster daemons run in a dedicated `Namespace` so that they are not accessible to users of the cluster, though, in some cases, users may install cluster daemons into their own `Namespaces`. When it comes time to monitor, upgrade, or otherwise maintain these daemons, they are maintained exactly like any other application running on the Kubernetes cluster. Running agents in this manner is more reliable, since they inherit all of the same capabilities that make running any other application in Kubernetes easier. It is also more consistent, since both agents and applications are monitored and maintained using the same tools.

In the following sections, we explore additional ways in which programs running on a Kubernetes cluster can extend or enhance that cluster. However, what distinguishes cluster agents or daemons from other extensions is that the capabilities they provide apply to all objects within a cluster or within a Namespace, without additional user interaction to enable them. They are enabled automatically and users often gain the functionality without even being aware that they are present.

Use Cases for Cluster Daemons

There are many different sorts of functionality that you might want to provide to a user automatically. A great example is automatic metrics collection from servers that expose Prometheus. When you run Prometheus within a Kubernetes cluster and configure it to do Kubernetes-based `Service` discovery, it operates as a cluster daemon and automatically scans all Pods in the cluster for metrics that it should ingest. It does this by watching the Kubernetes API server to discover any new Pods as they come and go. Thus, any application that is run within a Kubernetes cluster with a Prometheus cluster agent automatically has metrics collected without any configuration or enablement by the developer.

Another example of a cluster daemon is an agent that scans services deployed in the cluster for cross-site scripting (XSS) vulnerabilities. This cluster daemon again watches the Kubernetes API server for when new Ingress (HTTP load balancer) services are created. When such services are created, it automatically scans all paths in the service for XSS vulnerable web pages and sends a report to the user. Again, because it is provided by a cluster daemon, this functionality is inherited by developers who use the cluster without any requirement that they even know what XSS is or that the scanning is occuring until they deploy a service that has a vulnerability. We see how to build this example at the end of the section.

Cluster daemons are powerful, because they add automatic functionality. The less developers have to learn but can instead inherit automatically from their environment, the more likely their applications are to be reliable and secure.

Installing a Cluster Daemon

Installation of a cluster daemon is done via container images and Kubernetes configuration files. These configurations may be developed by the cluster administrator, provided by a package manager (like Helm), or supplied by the developer of the service (e.g., an open source project or independent software vendor). Typically, the cluster administrator uses the kubectl tool to install the cluster daemon on the cluster, possibly with some additional configuration information, such as a license key or Namespaces to scan. After it is installed, the daemon immediately starts operation on the cluster, and any subsequent upgrades, repair, or removal of the daemon are performed via Kubernetes configuration objects, just like any other application.

Operational Considerations for Cluster Daemons

Although the installation of a cluster daemon is generally trivial—often just a single command-line call—the operational complexity incurred by adding such a daemon can be quite significant. The automatic nature of cluster add-ons is a double-edged sword. Users will quickly come to rely on them, and thus the operational importance of cluster daemon add-ons can be significant. That is, while some of cluster daemons' value is derived from their transparent nature, users are unlikely to notice them failing. Imagine, for example, that your security regime is based on automated XSS scanning via a cluster daemon, and that daemon gets silently stuck. Suddenly, all XSS detection for your entire cluster may be disabled. Installation of a cluster daemon shifts the responsibility for the reliability of these systems from the developer to the cluster administrator. Generally, this is the right thing to do, since it centralizes knowledge of these extensions, and it allows for a single team to build services shared by a large number of other teams. But it is critical that cluster administrators know what they are signing up for. You cannot just install a cluster daemon on a whim or because of a user's request. You must be fully committed to operational management and support of that cluster daemon for the lifetime of the cluster.

Hands-On: Example of Creating a Cluster Daemon

Creating a cluster daemon doesn't need to be hard. In fact, a simple bash script that you might run from a single machine can easily be transformed into a cluster daemon. Consider, for example, the following script:

```
#!/bin/bash
for service in $(kubectl --all-namespaces get services | awk '{print $0}'); do
  python XssPy.py -u ${service} -e
done
```

This script lists all services in a cluster and then uses an open source XSS scanning script (*http://bit.ly/2P4XuH0*) to scan each service and print out the report.

To turn this into a cluster daemon, we simply need to place this script in a loop (with some delays, of course) and give it a way to report:

```
#!/bin/bash
# Start a simple web server
mkdir -p www
cd www
python -m SimpleHTTPServer 8080 &
cd ..

# Scan every service and write a report.
while true; do
  for service in $(kubectl --all-namespaces get services | awk '{print $0}'); do
    python XssPy.py -u ${service} -e > www/${service}-$(date).txt
  done
  # Sleep ten minutes between runs
  sleep 600
done
```

If you package this script up in a Pod and run it in your cluster, you will have a collection of XSS reports available from the Pod. Of course, to really productionize this, there are many other things that you might need, including uploading files to a central repository, or monitoring/alerting. But this example shows that building a cluster daemon does not have to be a complicated task for Kubernetes experts. A little shell script and a Pod are all you need.

Cluster Assistants

Cluster assistants are quite similar to cluster daemons, but unlike cluster daemons, in which functionality is automatically enabled for all users of the cluster, a cluster assistant requires the user to provide some configuration or other gesture to opt in to the functionality provided by the assistant. Rather than providing automatic experiences, cluster assistants provide enriched, yet easily accessible, functionality to users of the cluster, but it is functionality that the user must be aware of and must provide appropriate information to enable.

Use Cases for Cluster Assistants

The uses cases for cluster assistants are generally those in which a user wants to enable some functionality, but the work to enable the capabilities is significantly harder, slower, or more complicated and error prone than necessary. Given such a situation, it is the job of the assistant to help automate this process to make it easier, more automatic, and less likely to suffer from "cut and paste" or other configuration errors. Assistants simplify tedious or rote tasks in a cluster to make them easier to consume concepts.

As a concrete example of such a process, consider what is necessary to add an SSL certificate to an HTTP service in a Kubernetes cluster. First, a user must obtain a certificate. Although APIs, like Let's Encrypt, have made this significantly easier, it is still a nontrivial task, requiring a user to install tooling, set up a server, and claim a domain. However, after the certificate is obtained, you still aren't done. You need to figure out how to deploy it into your web server. Some developers may follow best practices and, knowing about Kubernetes Ingress, make a Kubernetes Secret, associating the certificate with the HTTP load balancer. But other developers may take the easy (and dramatically less secure) route and bake the certificate directly into their container image. Still others may balk at the complexity and decide that SSL isn't actually required for their use case.

Regardless of the outcome, the extra work by developers—and the different implementations of SSL—are unnecessary risks. Instead, the addition of a cluster assistant to automate the process of provisioning and deploying SSL certificates can reduce developer complexity and can ensure that all certificates in the cluster are obtained, deployed, and rotated in a manner that follows best practices. However, to operate correctly, the cluster assistant requires the knowlege and engagement of the end user of the cluster, in this case, the domain name for the certificate, and an explicit request for SSL to be attached to the load balancer via the cluster assistant. Such an assistant is implemented by the open source cert-manager project (*https://github.com/jetstack/cert-manager*).

For a cluster administrator, cluster assistants centralize knowledge and best practices, reduce questions from users by simplifying complex cluster configurations, and ensure that all services deployed to a cluster have a common look and feel.

Installing a Cluster Assistant

Because the difference between cluster assistants and cluster daemons comes from the pattern of interaction—not the implementation—the installation of a cluster assistant is more or less identical to the installation of a cluster daemon. The cluster assistant is packaged as a container image and deployed via standard Kubernetes API objects, like Deployments and Pods. Like cluster daemons, maintenance, operations, and removal of the cluster assistants are managed via the Kubernetes API.

Operational Considerations for Cluster Assistants

Like cluster daemons, cluster assistants need the cluster administrator to take on operational responsibility. Because the assistants hide complexity from the end user, meaning that the end user is ultimately unaware of the details of how a task like installing a certificate is actually implemented, it is critical that the assistants function correctly. The end user is unlikely to be able to achieve similar tasks on their own, due to lack of experience and knowledge. However, because the functionality is opt-in, a user is far more likely to notice that something isn't working. For example, the user requested an SSL certificate and it didn't arrive. However, this doesn't mean that the cluster administrator has less operational burden. You still should be proactively monitoring and repairing cluster assistant infrastructure, but someone is more likely to notice when things go wrong.

Hands-On: Example of Cluster Assistants

To make this a little bit more concrete, let's build an example cluster assistant that automatically adds authentication to a Kubernetes `Service`. The basic operation of this assistant is that it continuously scans the list of `Service` objects in your cluster looking for objects with a specific annotation key: `managing-k8s.io/authentication-secret`. It is expected that the value for this key points to a Kubernetes Secret that contains a *.htpasswd* file. For example:

```
kind: Service
metadata:
  name: my-service
  annotations:
    managing-k8s.io/authentication-secret: my-httpasswd-secret
...
```

When the cluster assistant finds such an annotation, it creates two new Kubernetes objects. First, it creates a `Deployment`, which contains a replicated `nginx` web server Pod. These Pods take the *.httpasswd* file that was referenced by the Secret in the annotation, and configure `nginx` as a reverse proxy, which forwards traffic on to `my-service` but requires a user and password as specified in the *.htpasswd* file. The cluster assistant also creates a Kubernetes `Service` named `authenticated-my-service` that directs traffic to this authentication layer. That way, a user can expose this authenticated service to the external world and have authentication without having to worry about how to configure `nginx`. Of course, basic authentication is a pretty simple example. You can easily imagine extending it to cover OAuth or other, more sophisticated, authentication endpoints.

Extending the Life Cycle of the API Server

The previous examples were applications that run on top of your cluster, but there are limits to what is possible with such cluster extensions. A deeper sort of extensibility comes from extending the behavior of the API server itself. These extensions can be applied to all API requests directly, as they are processed by the API server itself. This enables additional extensibility for your cluster.

Use Cases for Extending the API Life Cycle

Because API life cycle extensions exist in the path of the API server, you can use them to enforce requirements on all API objects that are created by the service. For example, suppose that you want to ensure that all container images that run in the cluster come from your company's private registry and that a naming convention is maintained. You might, for example, want all images to be of the form *registry.my-co.com/<team-name>/<server-name>:<git-hash>* where *registry.my-co.com* is a private image registry run by your company, *<team-name>* and *<server-name>* are well-known teams and applications built by those teams, and finally, <git-hash> is a source-control commit hash indicating the revision from which the image was built. Requiring such an image name ensures that developers don't store their production images on public (unauthenticated) image repositories, and the naming conventions ensure that any application (e.g., the XSS scanner we described earlier) has access to metadata that is needed to send notifications. Requiring the git-hash ensures that developers only build images from checked in (and therefore code-reviewed) source code and that it is easy to go from a running image to the source code that it is running.

To implement this functionality, we can register a custom admission controller. Admission controllers were described in "Life of a Request" on page 39. They are responsible for determining whether an API request is accepted (or admitted) into the API server. In this case, we can register an admission controller that is run for all API objects that contain an image field (Pods, Deployments, DaemonSets, Replica Sets, and StatefulSets). The admission controller introspects the image field in these objects and validates that they match the naming pattern just described and that the various components of the image name are valid (e.g., the team-name is associated with a known team, and the git-hash is one in a release branch of the team's repository).

Installing API Life Cycle Extensions

There are two parts to installing API life cycle extensions. The first is creating a Ser
vice to handle the webhook calls, and the second is creating a new Kubernetes API
object that adds the extension. To create the Service that handles the webhook calls
from the API server, you need to create a web service that can respond appropriately.
There are many ways to do this, from functions as a service (FaaS) from a cloud provider, to FaaS implementations on the cluster itself (e.g., OpenFaaS), to a standard
web application implemented in your favorite programming language. Depending on
the requirements for the webhook handler and the operations/cost requirements, you
can make different decisions. For example, using a cloud-based FaaS might be the
easiest in terms of setup and operations, but each invocation will cost some money.
On the other hand, if you already have an open source FaaS implementation running
on your cluster, that is a logical place to run your webhooks. But installing and maintaining an operational support system (OSS) FaaS might be more work than it's
worth, if you have only a few webhooks, and running a simple web server might be
the right choice. You need to make such choices, as your situations warrant.

Operational Considerations for Life Cycle Extensions

From an operational standpoint, there are two operational complexities to consider.
The first and more obvious complexity comes from having to run a Service to handle the webhook. The operational responsibility here varies, as described earlier,
depending on where you run the particular webhook. Regardless, you need to monitor your webhooks for at least application-level reliability (e.g., not returning 500s)
and perhaps more. The second operational complexity is more subtle, and it comes
from having your own code injected into the critical path for the API server. If you
implement a custom admission controller and it starts crashing and returning 500s,
all requests to the API server that use this admission controller will start failing. Such
an event could have significant impact on the correct operation of your cluster, and it
could cause a wide variety of failures that could affect the correct operation of applications deployed on top of the controller. In a less extreme case, your code could add
extra latency to the API calls that it affects. This added latency could cause bottle-
necks in other parts of the Kubernetes cluster (e.g., the controller manager or scheduler), or it might just make your cluster seem flaky or slow if your extension
occasionally runs slowly or fails. Whatever the case, placing code in the API server
call path should be done carefully and with monitoring, thought, and planning to
ensure that there are not any unanticipated consequences.

Hands-On: Example of Life Cycle Extensions

To implement an admission controller you need to implement the admission control
webhook. The admission control webhook receives an HTTP POST with a JSON body

that contains an `AdmissionReview`. You may find it helpful to explore type definitions in more detail (*http://bit.ly/2QmE7ti*).

Let's implement a simple JavaScript service that admits Pods.

```javascript
const http = require('http');

const isValid = (pod) => {
  // validate pod here
};

const server = http.createServer((request, response) => {
  var json = '';
  request.on('data', (data) => {
    json += data;
  });
  request.on('end', () => {
    var admissionReview = JSON.parse(json);
    var pod = admissionReview.request.object;

    var review = {
      kind: 'AdmissionReview',
      apiVersion: 'admission/v1beta1',
      response: {
        allowed: isValid(pod)
      }
    };
    response.end(JSON.stringify(review));
  });
});

server.listen(8080, (err) => {
  if (err) {
    return console.log('admission controller failed to start', err);
  }

  console.log('admission controller up and running.');
});
```

You can see that we take an `AdmissionReview` object, extract the Pod from the review, validate it, and then return an `AdmissionReview` object with a response filled in.

You can then register this dynamic admission controller with Kubernetes by creating the registration:

```yaml
apiVersion: admissionregistration.k8s.io/v1beta1
kind: ValidatingWebhookConfiguration
metadata:
  name: my-admission-controller
webhooks:
- name: my-web-hook
  rules:
  # register for create of v1/pod
```

```
- apiGroups:
  - ""
  apiVersions:
  - v1
  operations:
  - CREATE
  resources:
  - pods
clientConfig:
  service:
    # Send requests to a Service named 'my-admission-controller-service'
    # in the kube-system namespace
    namespace: kube-system
    name: my-admission-controller-service
```

As with all Kubernetes objects, you can instantiate this dynamic admission controller registration with `kubectl create -f <web-hook-yaml-file>`. But make sure that the right `Service` is up and running before you do so, or subsequent Pod creations may fail.

Adding Custom APIs to Kubernetes

Though we've shown you how to extend existing APIs, these modifications are limited to the set of APIs compiled into the API server. Sometimes, you want to add entirely new API resource types to your cluster. In particular, although Kubernetes comes with a rich set of API types that you can use to implement your application, sometimes you want to add new API types to the Kubernetes API. This dynamic type capability in Kubernetes allows you to take an existing cluster, with a collection of built-in API types, like Pods, `Services`, and Deployments, and add new types that largely look and feel exactly as if they had been built in. This sort of extensibility is quite flexible and powerful, but it is also the most abstract and complicated to understand. At the highest level, you can think of this sort of extension as adding new API objects to the Kubernetes API server—API objects that look as if they have been compiled into Kubernetes. All of the tooling for handling existing Kubernetes objects applies natively to these extensions.

Use Cases for Adding New APIs

Because custom API types are so flexible that they can literally represent any object, there are a large number of potential use cases. The following examples only just scratch the surface of these possibilities. In earlier sections, we discussed open source implementations of FaaS that run on top of Kubernetes. When a FaaS is installed on top of Kubernetes, it adds new functionality to the cluster. With this new functionality, you need an API to create, update, and delete functions in the FaaS. Although you could implement your own new API for this FaaS, you would have to implement many of the things (authorization, authentication, error handling, and more) that the

Kubernetes API server already has implemented for you. Consequently, it is far easier to model the functions provided by the FaaS as Kubernetes API extensions. Indeed, this is what many of the popular open source FaaS do. When you install one on Kubernetes, it turns around and registers new types with the Kubernetes API. After these new types have been registered, all of the existing Kubernetes tools (e.g., kubectl) apply directly to these new function objects. This familiarity means that, in many cases, users of extended clusters may not even notice that they are using API extensions.

Another popular use case for API extensions is the operator pattern championed by CoreOS. With an operator, a new API object is introduced into the cluster to represent the (formerly human) "operator" of a piece of software (e.g., a database administrator). To achieve this, a new API object is added to the Kubernetes API server that represents this "operated" piece of software. For example, you might add a MySQLData base object to Kubernetes via API extensions. When a user creates a new instance of a MySQLDatabase, the operator then uses this API object to instantiate a new MySQLDa tabase, including appropriate monitoring and online supervision to automatically keep the database running correctly. Thus, through operators and API extensibility, users of your cluster can directly instantiate databases instead of Pods that happen to run databases.

Custom Resource Definitions and Aggregated API Servers

Because both the API life cycle and the process of extending the API is technically complicated, Kubernetes actually implements two separate mechanisms for adding new types to the Kubernetes API. The first is known as CustomResourceDefinitions , and it involves using the Kubernetes API itself to add new types to Kubernetes. All of the storage and API serving associated with the new custom type are handled by Kubernetes itself. Because of this, custom resource definitions are by far a simpler way to extend the Kubernetes API server. On the other hand, because Kubernetes handles all of the extensibility, there are several limitations to these APIs. For example, it is difficult to perform validation and defaulting for APIs added by custom resource definitions; however, it is possible by combining custom resource definitions with a custom admission controller.

Because of these limitations, Kubernetes also supports API delegation, in which the complete API call, including the storage, of the resources is delegated to an alternate server. This enables the extension to implement an arbitrarily complex API, but it also comes with significant operational complexity, especially the need to manage your own storage. Because of this complexity, most API extensions use custom resource definitions. Describing how to implement delegated API servers is beyond the scope of this book, and the remainder of this section describes how to use Custom ResourceDefinitions to extend the Kubernetes API.

Architecture for Custom Resource Definitions

There are several different steps to implementing a custom resource definition. The first is the creation of the `CustomResourceDefinition` object itself. Custom resources are built-in Kubernetes objects with the new type definition. After a `CustomResource Definition` is created, the Kubernetes API server programs itself with a new API group and resource path in the API web server, as well as new handlers that know how to serialize and deserialize these new custom resources from Kubernetes storage. If all you want is a simple CRUD API, this may be sufficient. But in most cases, you want to actually do something when a user creates a new instance of your custom object. To do this, you need to combine the Kubernetes `CustomResourceDefinition` with a controller application that watches these custom definitions and then takes action based on resources that the user creates, updates, or destroys. In many cases, this application server is also the application that registers the new custom resource definition. Figure 13-1 diagrams this flow.

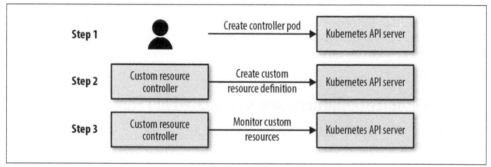

Figure 13-1. A diagram of the three steps in custom resource definition

The combination of a custom resource and a controller application is generally suffi‐cient for most applications, but you may want to add even more functionality to your API (e.g., precreate validation or defaulting). To do this, you can also add an admis‐sion controller for your newly defined custom resources that inserts itself in the API life cycle, as described in the Chapter 4, and adds these capabilities to your custom resource.

Installing Custom Resource Definitions

Like all of the extensions, the code needed to manage these custom resources is run on the Kubernetes cluster itself. The custom resource controller is packaged as a con‐tainer image and installed on the cluster using Kubernetes API objects. Because a cus‐tom resource is a more complicated extension, generally speaking, the Kubernetes configuration consists of multiple objects packaged into a single YAML file. In many cases, these files can be obtained from the open source project or software vendor supplying the extension. Alternately they can be installed via a package manager, like

---

Helm. As with all of the other extensions, monitoring, maintenance, and deletion of the custom resource API extensions occur using the Kubernetes API.

 When a CustomResourceDefinition is deleted, *all* of the corresponding resources are also deleted from the cluster's data store. They cannot be recovered. So, when deleting a custom resource, be careful and make sure to communicate with all end users of that resource before you delete the CustomResourceDefinition.

Operational Considerations for Custom Resources

The operational considerations of a custom resource are generally the same as for other extensions. You are adding an application to your cluster that users will rely on and that needs to be monitored and managed. Furthermore, if your extension also uses an admission controller, the same operational concerns for admission controllers apply, as well. However, in addition to the complexities described earlier, there is significant additional complexity for custom resource definitions—they use the same storage associated with all of the built-in Kubernetes API objects. As a result, it is possible to impact your API server and cluster operation by storing objects too large and/or numerous in the API server using custom resources. In general, API objects in Kubernetes are intended to be simple configuration objects. They're not intended to represent large data files. If you find yourself storing large amounts of data in custom API types, you should probably consider installing some sort of dedicated key-value store or other storage API.

Summary

Kubernetes is great—not just because of the value of the core APIs it provides, but also because of all of the dynamic extension points that allow users to customize their clusters to suit their needs. Whether it is via dynamic admission controllers to validate API objects, or new custom resource definitions, there is a rich ecosystem of external add-ons that you can use to build a customized experience that fits your users' needs perfectly. And, if a necessary extension doesn't exist, the details in this chapter should help you design and build one.

## CHAPTER 14

Conclusions

Kubernetes is a powerful tool that enables users to decouple from operating machines and focus on the core operations of their applications. This enables users to build, deploy, and manage applications at scale significantly more easily and efficiently. Of course, to achieve this, someone has to actually deploy and manage the Kubernetes cluster itself; the Kubernetes application is their focus.

We hope that this overview of the Kubernetes API and architecture and topics like RBAC, upgrades, monitoring, and extending Kubernetes give you the knowledge necessary to successfully deploy and operate Kubernetes so that your users don't have to.

Index

data storage (see storage)
debugging
    API server, 46-48
    audit logs, 47
    basic logs, 47
    ClusterRole resource type, 95
    kubectl requests, 48
decentralized system design, 22
declarative configuration, 21
Deployments (Deployment objects), 15
design principles, Kubernetes
    API-driven interactions, 25
    Unix modularity philosophy, 25
dex, 84
disaster recovery, 141-147
    application data recovery, 142
    Ark for, 145
    etcd backup, 144
    high availability and, 141
    Kubernetes architecture and, 3
    local data, 143
    state restoration, 142
    worker nodes, 143
DNS
    KubeDNS server, 29
    namespaces and, 14
    Service discovery and, 119
    Service object and, 12
dynamic admission controllers, 107-113
    about, 107-110
    mutating controllers, 110-113
    validating controllers, 108-110
dynamic/implicit grouping, 23

E

Elasticsearch, 134
encryption, Secret data and, 66
environment variables, 120
etcd, 27
    backup, 144
    cluster size and performance, 141
    kubeadm and, 65-67
    Secret data, 66
extending Kubernetes, 4, 149-161
    cluster assistants, 152-155
    cluster daemons, 150-152
    custom APIs, 158-161
    Custom Resource Definitions and aggrega-
        ted API servers, 159-161

external representation, 37

F

fluentd daemon, 132

G

general availability, 37
grouping, implicit/dynamic, 23

H

head nodes
    about, 26
    API server, 27
    components, 26
    controller manager, 28
    etcd system, 27
    scheduler, 27
high availability
    control plane and, 70
    disaster recovery and, 141
HTTP load balancing, 16
HTTP paths, 32

I

image registry, 9
imperative configuration, 21
implicit/dynamic grouping, 23
independent reconciliation loops, 22
InfluxDB, 133
Ingress API, 16
installation
    add-ons, 69
    API life cycle extensions, 156
    certificate generation, 65
    cluster assistants, 153
    cluster daemons, 151
    CNI plug-in, 69
    control plane, 62-68
    kubeadm, 59-62
    kubeadm phases feature, 70
    Kubernetes, 59-73
    preflight checks, 64
    upgrades, 71-73
    worker nodes, 68
internal representation, 38
isolation, in Kubernetes context, 8

J

Job object, 18
job scheduling (see scheduling)

K

kube-proxy, 28, 117-119
kubeadm, 59-62
    and highly available control plane, 70
    certificate generation, 65
    configuration, 63
    etcd, 65-67
    kubeconfig file generation, 67
    kubelet and, 61-62
    phases feature, 70
    preflight checks, 64
    requirements, 60
    upgrade installation, 71-73
kubeadm API, 63
kubeconfig files, 67, 85-87
kubectl command-line tool
    API discovery, 33
    debugging API server with, 48
KubeDNS server, 29
kubelet, 28, 61-62
Kubernetes (generally)
    API, 10-18
    architecture, 21-30
    containers, 7-9
    design concepts, 21-24
    design principles, 25
    extending (see extending Kubernetes)
    overview, 7-19
    Services, 12
    storage, 12-14
    Volumes, 13

L

label queries, 15
label selectors, 53
labels
    annotations vs., 24
    basics, 15
LimitRange controller, 106
liveness checks, 10
load balancing, 10
    Ingress API, 16
    Service, 12
logging

API server, 46-48
    audit logs, 47
    basic logs, 47
    monitoring vs., 129
    streaming logs, 138
    verbosity level adjustment, 47

M

metrics, for disaster recovery and monitoring, 3
modularity (Unix philosophy), 25
monitoring, 127-139
    aggregating metrics and logs from multiple
        sources, 131
    alerting and, 138
    blackbox, 137
    getting data from cluster and applications,
        129-131
    goals for, 127-129
    layered approach to, 134-136
    logging vs., 129
    of applications, 136
    of Kubernetes components in cluster, 136
    of machines, 135
    stack construction, 129-134
    storing data for retrieval and querying, 133
    streaming logs, 138
    visualizing/interacting with data, 134
    whitebox vs. blackbox, 128, 135
monolithic system design, 22
mutating admission controllers, 107, 110-113

N

Namespaces (Namespace object), 8, 14, 32
networking, 115-125
    Container Network Interface, 115-117
    kube-proxy, 117-119
    policy enforcement, 121-123
    Service discovery, 119-121
    service mesh, 123
NetworkPolicy resource, 121-123
node affinity, 54-56
node selectors, 53
    and node affinity, 54-56
    labels and, 15
node taints (see taints)

O

one-time (batch) workloads, 18

open container initiative (OCI) standard, 8
OpenAPI, 36
OpenID Connect (OIDC), 80-82, 84
optimistic concurrency, 27
optimistically concurrent updates, 43
orchestration system, 9

P

pause containers, 116
persistent volumes, 143
phases (kubeadm feature), 70
Pod selectors, 15
Pod, as basic object, 10
PodSecurityPolicies controller, 102-104
policy enforcement
    networking and, 121-123
    RoleBinding and ClusterRoleBinding, 96
predicates, 50
priorities (priority functions), 50
private registries, 9
probe monitoring (see blackbox monitoring)
Prometheus, 4
    and off-the-shelf software, 132
    as pull-based aggregator, 131
    integrating new application metrics with,
        130
    machine metrics monitoring with, 135
    operating as cluster daemon, 150
Protocol Buffers, 45
public registries, 9
pull aggregation, 131
push-based monitoring system, 131

Q

quotas, ResourceQuota controller and, 104-106

R

RBAC (see role-based access control)
readiness checks, 10
reconciliation loops, 22
replica sets, 11
request management, API server, 38-45
    admission control, 40
    alternate encodings, 44
    authentication, 39
    HTTP response codes, 45
    optimistically concurrent updates, 43
    RBAC/authorization, 40

specialized requests, 41
stages of a request, 39-45
types of requests, 38
validation, 40
watch operations, 43
request validation, 40
ResourceQuota controller, 104-106
REST, semantics of, 91
RESTful APIs, 91
Role resource type, 94-96
role-based access control (RBAC)
    authorization and, 93-98
    in request processing, 40
    Role and ClusterRole, 94-96
    RoleBinding and ClusterRoleBinding, 96
    testing authorization, 98
RoleBinding resource, 96

S

sandbox interfaces, 116
scheduled components, 29
    Heapster, 29
    KubeDNS server, 29
ScheduledJob object, 18
scheduler, 27
scheduling, 49-57
    algorithm for, 51
    conflicts, 52
    node selectors, 53
    overview, 49
    predicates, 50
    priority functions, 50
    process, 50-53
    taints and tolerations, 56
    tools for customizing, 53-57
Secret data, 66
Secret type, 13
security, 3
    (see also authentication, authorization)
    clusters and, 3
Service discovery, 119-121
    DNS and, 119
    environment variables, 120
    monitoring applications with, 136
service mesh, 117, 123
ServiceAccount, 87-89, 97
Services
    and Pod selectors, 15
    basics, 12

sets, implicit/dynamic grouping, 23
state restoration and disaster recovery, 142
StatefulSets, 17
storage
    basics, 12-14
    ConfigMaps, 13
    Elasticsearch, 134
    for retrieval and querying, 133
    InfluxDB, 133
    Secret type, 13
    Volumes, 13
storage representation, 38
streaming logs, 138

T

taints (node taints), 56
    control plane nodes and, 68
    toleration and, 56
time series, 133
toleration, 56
translation, API, 37

U

Unix, 25
upgrades, installation of, 71-73
user management, 75-89, 76

(see also authentication)
users, in Kubernetes context, 76

V

validating admission controllers, 107-108
validation, in request processing, 40
version skew, 25

W

watch API, 43
watch protocol, 27
Webhook authentication, 82-84
webhooks (see dynamic admission controllers)
whitebox monitoring, 128, 135
worker nodes
    about, 26
    disaster recovery, 143
    installation, 68

X

X.509 client certificates, 78-80

Y

YAML encoding, 45

About the Authors

Brendan Burns is a cofounder of the Kubernetes open source container management platform. He is currently a distinguished engineer at Microsoft, running the Azure Resource Manager and Azure Container Service teams. Before Microsoft, he was a senior staff engineer on the Google Cloud Platform. Prior to working in cloud, he developed web search backends that helped power Google Search. He is also a former professor of computer science at Union College in Schenectady, New York. Brendan received a PhD in computer science from the University of Massachusetts Amherst and a BA from Williams College.

Craig Tracey has helped build the infrastructure that powers the internet every day for the past 20 years. In this time, he has had the opportunity to develop everything from kernel device drivers to massive-scale cloud storage services and even a few distributed compute platforms. Now as a software engineer turned field engineer at Heptio, by teaching the principles of cloud-native architectures through code, he helps organizations accelerate their adoption of Kubernetes.

Based in Boston, Massachusetts, Craig loves playing hockey in his free time and enjoys exploring Europe. Craig holds a BS in computer science from Providence College.

Colophon

The animal on the cover of *Managing Kubernetes* is the violet crossfish (*Uraster violacea*). Found on the coasts of Great Britain, it can range in color from bright orange to deep red, with blue spots that blend with the warmer colors toward its extremities, culminating in a brilliant purple at the end of each ray. Generally, it has been observed to four to five inches in length, and like the common starfish, has a broad, omnivorous diet, including algae, sponges, snails, bivalves, and other small plants and creatures.

Many of the animals on O'Reilly covers are endangered; all of them are important to the world. To learn more about how you can help, go to *animals.oreilly.com*.

The cover image is from Edward Forbes' *A History of British Starfish and other Animals of the Class Echinodermata*. The cover fonts are URW Typewriter and Guardian Sans. The text font is Adobe Minion Pro; the heading font is Adobe Myriad Condensed; and the code font is Dalton Maag's Ubuntu Mono.

Learn from experts.
Find the answers you need.

Sign up for a **10-day free trial** to get **unlimited access** to all of the content on Safari, including Learning Paths, interactive tutorials, and curated playlists that draw from thousands of ebooks and training videos on a wide range of topics, including data, design, DevOps, management, business—and much more.

Start your free trial at:
oreilly.com/safari

(No credit card required.)